FREELANCE PHOTOGRAPHERS' BRITAIN

FREELANCE PHOTOGRAPHERS' BRITAIN

Kevin MacDonnell

BFP BOOKS London

British Library Cataloguing in Publication Data:

MacDonnell, Kevin
Freelance photographers' Britain.
1. Photography——Landscapes 2. Travel photography——Great Britain 3. Great Britain——Description and travel——1971– ——Views
I. Title
778.9'36'0941 TR660

ISBN 0–907297–11–0

First published 1988

Cover pictures by Edmund Nägele, FRPS

Published by BFP Books, Focus House, 497 Green Lanes, London N13 4BP.
Printed and bound in Great Britain by Butler & Tanner Ltd
Frome and London

Contents

Introduction

A visiting American photographer said to me the other day: "You don't know how lucky you are here in Britain. Back home I can leave a small town, drive 400 miles to another and find the same scenery, the same houses and shops, the same people, the same way of life—I might just as well not have bothered. In Britain an hour's drive can bring a complete change in every respect, almost as though you'd entered another country. How can anyone here ever say they've run out of subjects?"

I've never thought much about it but he was absolutely right. No matter how familiar and boring your surroundings, fresh and interesting material lies only a bus ride away. This small country is packed with beautiful, extraordinary, fascinating (and saleable) pictures waiting to be taken. All you have to do is to find them and photograph them in an interesting way, and the purpose of this book is to help you to do so.

Though stress is laid on taking pictures that will be reproduced in print—in other words ones that will sell—it is important to produce results that you yourself like and find interesting. Apart from the satisfaction this brings, pictures taken against your better judgement simply because you think someone else will like them are rarely successful—good photography reflects the interests, ideas and personality of the person behind the camera. An experienced picture editor looking at a photo often knows who has taken it without looking at the caption, because the cameraman has developed his own individual style, his own way of looking at things. Study the work of other photographers but don't copy them—try to say something fresh and different about every subject you record.

Photographically speaking Silbury Hill in Wiltshire, the largest man-made mound in Europe, is not very interesting in itself so you have to find a way of introducing some visual impact. My solution was to use a 17 mm lens and concentrate on the close-up cornfield in the foreground and the vast area of sky above. Super-wide lenses always give a sense of movement to clouds and can transform an otherwise very static subject into a lively one.

The nearest corn was eighteen inches away, the clouds were at infinity so the lens was closed down to f16. This called for a shutter speed of 1/30th on FP4 but there was little danger of camera shake with a lens of this focal length.

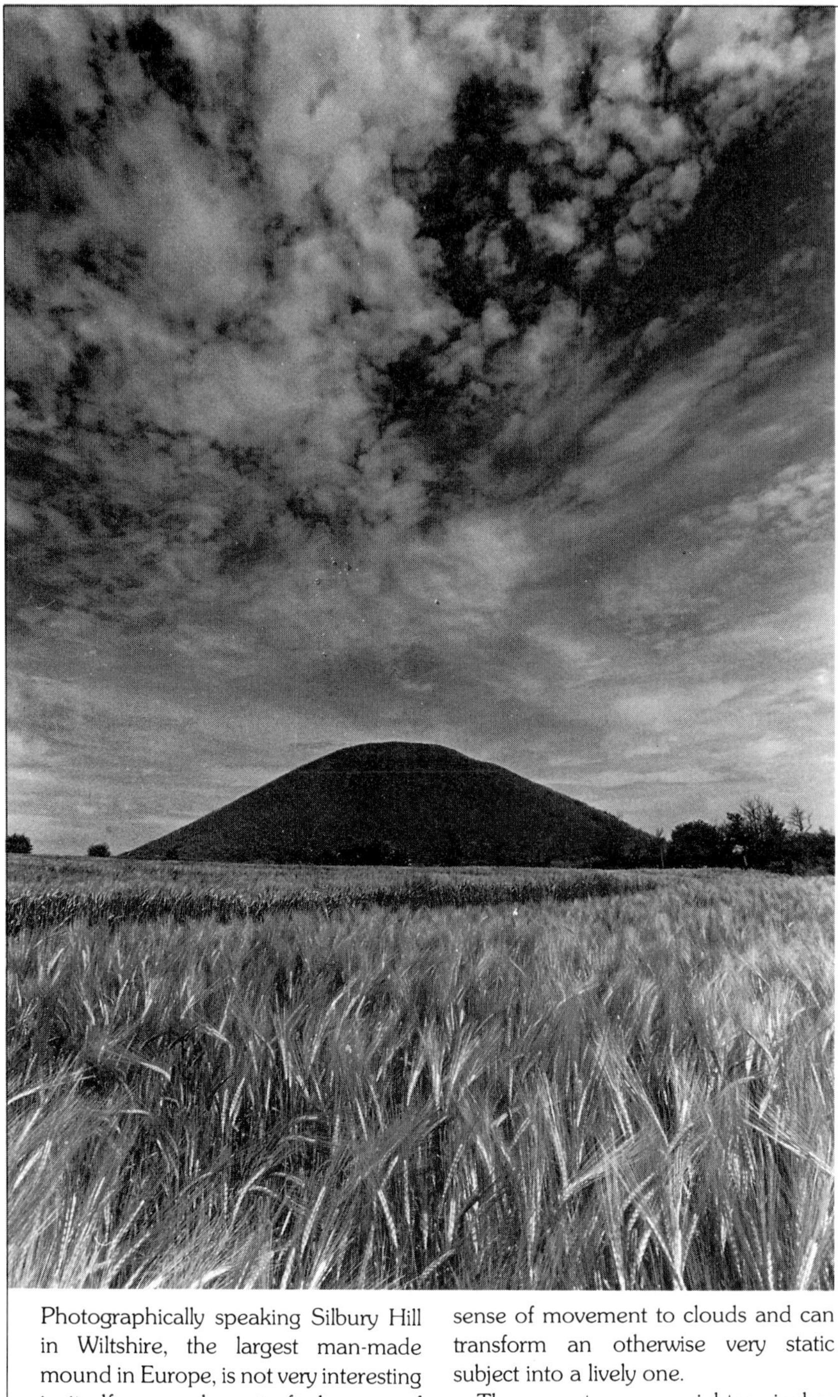

Choosing the Right Equipment

There is no such thing as a universal camera, one that will give the best possible result with every type of subject. They all without exception have advantages and disadvantages, and your choice will depend on the kind of photography that most interests you, your temperament, your physique and the compromises you are prepared to make. A picture of a thatched cottage taken to sell to a calendar publisher will be best taken with one kind of camera, whereas street market photography calls for a completely different instrument. However, it would be a fundamental mistake for the photographer who only works at weekends to keep switching cameras; it will take him all his time to become familiar with a single type.

To a large extent the difference between the full-time professional and the part-timer is that the former uses his camera so often that he soon stops thinking about it. His hands operate the controls without any conscious thought, leaving his mind free to concentrate on the things that really matter, the lighting, camera angle, composition and so on. The occasional photographer on the other hand, has to drag his attention away from the subject in order to think about the mechanical operation of the camera, and the picture often suffers as a result. It's bad enough if he uses just one type of camera, but if he tries to operate several in an attempt to get the best possible result every time he will never get to the stage where his hands move of their own accord.

My advice is to buy as good and as reliable a camera as you can afford and then to keep it and use it until you reach the stage when you no longer think about it. This may take years and your camera may eventually become "obsolete"—in other words unfashionable—but this is unimportant. Learning to use a new camera automatically is such a traumatic business for a busy professional that I know some who would sooner change their wives than their equipment! If you see a group of pressmen at work for instance, you'll probably notice that many of their cameras would be looked on as hopelessly out of date by the average amateur. They are, however, utterly reliable and over the years have become an extension of the photographer's mind.

35 mm Single Lens Reflexes

Easy to operate and carry, the 35 mm SLR can produce a high proportion of technically satisfactory results even in comparatively unskilled hands. Within its limitations it is an ideal instrument for the general purpose photography of Britain and is used by the great majority of advanced amateurs and by many professionals. However, when taking the more static subjects it cannot give the quality of the larger formats.

The first popular 35mm SLR was the pre-war Kine Exakta, built with strength and precision, which had for its day many advanced features but suffered from one fundamental disadvantage. The finder was the "waist-level" type which reversed the picture left-to-right when the camera was held horizontally and turned it upside down as well when vertical pictures were being taken, making upright compositions almost impossible. However in spite of this snag the Exakta was the basis for all modern 35mm SLRs.

Nearly all the modern technical advances were introduced especially for this type of camera—zoom lenses, pentaprisms, through-the-lens metering, electronic shutters, automation, auto-focusing, power wind, etc.—and today the choice of models is bewildering, with many new ones coming on the market every year all claiming to be an advance on anything previously available. For our purpose, that of recording Britain, the requirements are not novelty or even an advanced electronic specification but reliability, simplicity of use and the ability to produce results of high quality. A twenty-five year old Nikon F that is in good condition—probably having seen only occasional use in the hands of an amateur rather than having been used continually by a professional—may well give you sharper pictures than some modern cameras of equivalent price, and in addition will be rugged enough to stand up to the hard use it will inevitably receive in your hands. Don't confuse the latest with the best.

For the kind of pictures we are going to take the more simple the camera is to operate the better. A high-tech multi-mode program is not really necessary and may indeed make our photography more difficult. Let's consider what is really necessary and what is merely a selling point.

The Shutter

Most modern "automatic" cameras are fitted with electronic shutters. Battery operated, they have a stepless range of speeds and are set according to the strength of the light entering the lens, thus theoretically giving exactly the right exposure. Easy to mass-produce, they are accurate and reliable while the battery is working. However, since the life of a battery is limited most serious cameras have a mechanical back-up speed to keep you going when the battery fails, as it always does when you are in remote country on an important assignment (of course, one should always carry a spare but it is only too easy for this to deteriorate and be useless when needed). This back-up speed should be fast enough to let you hand-hold the camera safely—1/125th is usable, 1/60th is not. The more professional and expensive cameras have a whole range of mechanical back-up speeds, perhaps from 1/125th to 1/1000th.

Mechanical shutters which instead of being stepless are set to individual speeds are just as satisfactory, and from the practical point of view (and if you are taking pictures for money theory soon takes a back seat to practice) it will make little difference which type you choose. A few mechanical shutters are fitted to "automatic" cameras but they are more usually seen on manually-operated ones.

A range of speeds from 1 to 1/1000th of a second will cover all your needs, most of your pictures being taken between 1/60th and 1/500th. The higher the speed at which

Throughout photography the constant problem is to produce a feeling of depth, of realism, the classic method being to have something close to the camera, something in the middle distance and to have the main subject in the background. Here the two children lead into the picture (had they been running towards the camera the effect would have been spoilt) and the trees funnel your vision towards the sunlit buildings of Greenwich. Having selected your camera angle you often have to wait patiently for the right people to arrive to bring life to the picture, but eventually they always turn up.

the shutter synchronises with flash the better since it makes it easier to use flash out of doors.

The Body

At one time SLRs intended for serious work were large, heavy, all-metal affairs designed to last forever. They could be easily gripped and their weight gave them a useful stability at low shutter speeds, but since the lenses were equally massive an outfit weighed a lot and could become tiring to carry.

Then came the Olympus OM–1, astonishingly light and compact, and every designer started to follow the trend, some using plastic and over-thin metal to cut down the weight. For amateur use these were satisfactory, but many could not stand up to professional treatment. These days most manufacturers have settled on a compromise and modern cameras are large enough to hold firmly but light enough to carry without effort.

However, the choice of a camera is very much an individual matter. Many people who earn their living with one are prepared to sacrifice compactness and portability for ruggedness and an easy grip; others who have to carry their outfits a long way appreciate lightness. Neither type is better than the other; they simply represent different compromises.

For some of the work we are going to do a power wind or a motor drive can be a handicap. They are mainly intended for sports photographers who can fire a burst at an action sequence in the hope that one frame will have captured the decisive moment (though many experienced workers claim they often miss it and prefer to choose the moment to release the shutter themselves). They are also useful to pressmen, who when working in a crowd have to hold their camera in the air and shoot blind over the heads. The more extrovert amateurs who like to be both seen and heard when taking pictures appreciate the noise of the motor and the impression of professionalism they think it gives, but when photographing the people of Britain one should be as silent and as invisible as possible.

For the same reason it is wise to choose a mirror/shutter mechanism that does not attract attention when the release is pressed. Every make of camera has its own distinctive sound; I once knew a Japanese designer who could identify any make of SLR blindfold, just by listening to the noise it made. It is not so much the volume of sound that matters so much as the quality, some cameras making a sharp "clack" that causes heads to turn while others make an equally loud but duller noise that is ignored. If you are going to concentrate on inanimate subjects the sound of course does not matter, but as soon as you start to photograph people it becomes important.

Lens Mounts and Focusing

On the dealer's counter almost any type of lens mount seems efficient and easy to handle but once in the field you may find yourself having to change lenses with cold, stiff fingers in poor light. The tiny red dot that some manufacturers think sufficient to position the lens correctly then becomes almost invisible and small lens release catches become hard to operate. The more obvious and simple the lens-changing mechanism the better—I like the lens barrel to have a raised red knob to indicate the correct position for insertion into the lens mount, the lens locking into position after having been given a quarter turn: even in the dark the system can be easily operated.

Though tastes vary, for general purposes the standard focusing screen consisting of a split-image rangefinder surrounded by a microprism circle is probably the most useful, the rangefinder being used if the subject has straight lines, focusing perhaps on a tree trunk in a landscape or an eyelid in a close-up portrait, while the microprism lets you focus on continuous tones. Some workers prefer an uncluttered screen of plain etched glass, but the rangefinder lets you focus very rapidly.

Automatic focusing is really unnecessary when you are photographing a static subject and have plenty of time, since the human eye is capable of slightly greater accuracy in these circumstances than the electronic mechanism, but for unposed portraits and for any subject where rapid focusing is essential it can be invaluable. Two types are available; one has the electronics built into the camera body, resulting in lenses that are light and uncluttered, the other type has the mechanism and batteries in the lens, making it a completely independent unit.

The argument in favour of the former is that the lenses appear and are handled normally. You of course have to buy the AF (autofocusing) lenses appropriate to the particular make of camera you are using, but since the operating mechanism is in the camera body and not in the lens barrel they are comparatively light and inexpensive.

However, more and more independent lens manufacturers are producing lenses with built-in auto-focusing that can be used with almost any make of ordinary camera so there is no need to buy a new body. Most designers are concentrating on medium and long focus types since auto-focusing is not so useful with wide angle lenses that have great depth of field, and many photographers are adding one to their existing outfits for use with suitable subjects.

Whichever type is preferred it is essential that there should be a lock on the focusing. The main part of the picture may well be to one side rather than in the central area on which the lens focuses itself, so having centralised the subject and let the lens focus on it the lock should be operated while the picture is re-composed.

It is also highly desirable that the lens should have "follow-focus"; the ability to stay continually in focus on a moving object. If you are photographing, say, a village band marching towards you, an experienced worker using an ordinary manual-focus camera will pre-focus on the spot which he knows will be correct, pressing the release when the band reaches it, but it is certainly more easy to view the band on the finder screen and to take the picture when the composition is at its best, knowing the result will be sharp.

Auto-focusing and zooms go together extremely well, removing one of the main objections to this type of lens. When used on a manual-focusing camera even experienced photographers, having focused and arranged the picture, find the temptation to adjust the composition slightly by altering the focal length and to then check the focusing almost irresistable, often missing the crucial moment as they do so. With auto-focusing the camera handles the focusing for you, leaving you free to concentrate on the single operation of setting the focal length.

Will auto-focusing help you to take better pictures of Britain? At least 90% of the pictures we will take could be produced equally well by a manually-focused lens, but on occasion the ability to obtain sharp pictures of moving objects, the help it gives with unposed portraits and the way in which it makes zoom lenses easy to handle can be invaluable. But it is by no means an essential.

Exposure

You can produce satisfactory prints from negatives that are a stop under or two stops over-exposed, but colour transparency material calls for much greater accuracy. You can make good printing plates from a slide that is half or even one stop under-exposed but as soon as the highlights lose detail due to over-exposure (half a stop at most) the plate-maker cannot get a good result.

It really isn't difficult to expose correctly, but in an attempt to substitute electronics for thought the manufacturers sometimes go to extreme lengths in order to cover every possible situation. Eight or even ten modes (exposure systems) are not uncommon and the problem of choosing the best one to use is far greater than that of deciding on the correct stop/speed combination.

All modern 35mm SLRs have a TTL (through-the-lens) exposure system, a light-sensitive cell inside the camera measuring the brightness of the area of the subject included by the lens—no matter what its focal length the meter only considers the picture on the screen. The majority of cameras couple the meter to an "automatic exposure system". With some the photographer chooses and sets the stop while the camera sets the shutter speed that will expose the film accurately (aperture priority); with others the user sets the speed and the camera sets the stop (shutter priority).

Both systems are equally efficient, since if having set the stop with an aperture priority camera the shutter speed indicated is not fast enough to avoid camera shake you simply open up to a larger aperture. If, on the other hand, with shutter priority you feel the aperture is too large to give enough depth of field you lower the speed until it is. It really doesn't make much difference which type you use.

The third automatic system is known as "program", the camera selecting both the stop and the speed without any thought or control on the part of the photographer. It usually works well, and when combined with auto-focus the operator simply composes the subject on the screen, presses the release and knows he will get a sharp, correctly exposed result. However, the experienced photographer has a strong sense of unease at not knowing either the aperture or the speed at which he is working, and though in theory he should appreciate being able to concentrate his mind on the elements of the picture that really matter—lighting, camera angle, timing and so on—most prefer aperture or shutter priority.

A few metering systems take their reading evenly from the whole of the picture area but most are "centre weighted", the main part of the reading being taken from the central area with a lower proportion from the edges. The presumption is that the main part of the subject will occupy the centre of the frame which is probably true with most subjects. However if, for instance, you are taking landscapes with large sky areas, the kind of thing you get in East Anglia or the Romney Marsh, the foreground may well be under-exposed. This can be overcome if the camera has an "exposure lock", the camera being tilted down a little to reduce the sky area, the exposure locked and the picture being re-composed before the shutter is released.

Alternatively you can increase or reduce the exposure set automatically by using the exposure compensation dial, which usually adjusts the exposure by up to two stops. However, they are fiddling little devices to use and there is a very real danger that you will forget to reset them after you have taken the picture, with the result that the remainder of the film is incorrectly exposed.

When photographing very tall buildings, the kind you find in modern city centres for instance, it is often impossible to include the whole of them without tilting the camera. If the verticals converge slightly the result is irritating and can make the picture unsaleable. The answer is to fit a lens that includes the widest possible angle, preferably one with a focal length between 21 and 17 mm if you are using a 35 mm camera, get close to the subject and tilt boldly. The result will be dramatic and will add to the impression of height.

Because of these snags many landscape photographers prefer a non-automatic SLR such as the classic Olympus OM–1 or the Pentax K1000 in which the exposure is set by manually lining up a needle. To avoid too much influence from the sky the camera is tilted down while the needle is positioned, then raised before taking the picture. With other cameras using a similar system the needle is replaced by a column of lights, but most people feel more at ease positioning a needle even though in theory a galvanometer system is not as shock-proof as the solid-state electronics of the light column.

Since most automatic cameras have a "manual" setting it is common practice to work on "automatic" for the majority of subjects, switching to manual for landscapes or subjects with over-large shadow or highlight areas. It is easy to become obsessed with exposure measurement, so it is worth remembering that perhaps 95% of your subjects will have a fairly even distribution of light and dark tones and will consequently be handled perfectly by the automatic setting. It is better to concentrate your mind on the subject rather than on subtle differences in exposure measurement.

Any competent photographer should be able to set the exposure accurately in normal circumstances without the use of any meter at all so that he can go on working if it fails. All you have to do is to set the shutter speed as closely as possible to the ASA speed of the film (if it is 125 ASA the shutter is set at 1/125th; if 400 ASA, 1/500th and so on) while the stop is set at f16. With bright sunshine coming from behind you or at up to 45° from one side the exposure will be correct: if a light haze covers the sun and the edges of shadows soften, open up to f11; when light cloud causes shadows to become thin, f8; when cloud is heavy enough to make the shadows disappear, f5.6. These are your basic settings—any speed/stop combination that gives the same exposure can of course be used.

Though the owners of 35 mm SLRs invariably use through-the-lens metering, many professional cameras have no built-in metering at all, a separate handheld meter being used instead. These are broadly divided into two types, the selenium models that need no batteries and the CdS and Silicon ones that do. The advantages of the selenium meters are that they are permanently ready for use, there being no danger of battery failure, and in the case of the Weston and EuroMaster models, extreme accuracy. They work well in normal lighting but are not as sensitive as the battery operated types, some of which can operate in moonlight.

Whichever kind you use, consistently accurate results can be obtained, especially when using colour transparency material, by placing a white diffuser (called an "Invercone" in the Weston series) over the light-sensitive cell and then pointing the meter at the source of light which outdoors is, of course, the sun. You have to check that the light falling on the place where you are standing is similar to that on the subject (watch out for passing cloud shadows) but given that, you will find your transparencies have highlights of exactly the correct density, the tone range of the emulsion taking care of the shadows. This is the exposure-measuring system used in the film business, where an error can cost many thousands of pounds.

35 mm Interchangeable Lens Rangefinder Cameras

For many years the only 35 mm rangefinder cameras of professional quality to be marketed have been the Leica M series. They are expensive, even ancient secondhand ones holding

Trying out an inexpensive Agfa camera with auto exposure and an f2.8 lens I wanted to find out how it would handle low light subjects. Using 400 ASA film and with the lens at open aperture the exposure needed was too long for the camera to be safely hand held, so I rated the film at 1600 ASA and prolonged the development time to obtain a negative of normal density. Just how much increase in development is needed depends on the particular make of film and developer you are using—the instructions have to be followed with a fair degree of accuracy. Some films are much more easily push-processed than others but even with 400 ASA E6 colour reversal marterial you should be able to obtain a two stop increase without much loss in quality. However the results will never be as good as if the film had been rated at 400 ASA and processed normally.

On the other hand the technique allows any camera with an f2.8 lens to be used as though the lens had an aperture of f1.4, though with greater depth of field.

If you are going to include some foreground object to give a feeling of depth to the picture be bold about it, not halfhearted. Wide angle lenses (in this case a 28mm) and a small stop (f11 was used here) will give the necessary allover sharpness, though the depth of field scale will of course have to be used. Focus first of all on the nearest object and then set the scale so that the depth of field runs from this distance to infinity, presuming the furthest object is far away.

their price, but when fitted with the 50 mm f2 Summicron lens will give sharper results than any other 35 mm camera. The reasons for this are (1) there is no rising mirror or automatic diaphragm stop-down so vibration is at a minimum; all that moves when you press the release is the exceptionally smooth and silent shutter. (2) Since the lens designer does not have to leave extra space behind the rear element and the film in which the mirror can move, he is free to compute the best possible design. (3) The rangefinder is very accurate and much easier to use with lenses having a focal length of 50 mm or less than the focusing screen of an SLR.

The disadvantages are that the basic camera cannot be used with lenses with a focal length greater than 135 mm; the bright frame in the finder that indicates the area covered by the lens becomes very small with long focus ones; accessories, even simple ones like hoods and filters, are expensive; zoom lenses cannot be used.

The silent shutter makes them ideal cameras for unposed portraiture, a basic outfit is easily carried, they are pleasant and satisfying cameras to use and though the initial cost is high they will last indefinitely.

35 mm Compact Cameras

Though the majority of these are intended for fun photography there are a few, costing about the same as an average SLR, which are capable within their limitations of turning out professional results. Nearly all have automatic infra-red focusing (a different system to that used on SLRs, which operate by detecting the maximum contrast of the image) and the cheapest will only set the lens to a few fixed distances, depending on the depth of field of the semi-wide angle lens (usually about 38 mm). The top quality models have perhaps eleven or twelve focus settings, enough to give good sharpness with all subjects.

From our point of view their great advantage is that they can be carried in a large pocket, are always ready for use and allow a fleeting picture to be recorded without delay since they have "programmed" exposure setting as well as auto-focus. For town use they can be very useful provided you can get close enough to the subject to fill the frame (remembering the semi-wide lens). For occasions when you have time to think and compose the subject carefully, however, an SLR will give better results.

Medium Format Cameras

These include the 6 × 4.5 cm, 6 × 6 cm, 6 × 7 cm and 6 × 9 cm formats and are widely used by professionals. The main reason for this is that if you make a 10″ × 8″ print from a 35 mm negative the minimum degree of enlargement, presuming the subject was perfectly composed, is × 8; with a 6 × 6 cm negative it will be about × 4½. As a result a medium format print or transparency normally has better "quality" (a rather vague term which probably means a combination of sharpness and the ability to record small differences in tone) than that produced by a 35 mm camera, though on occasion the latter can come very close.

There are publishers who refuse to consider 35 mm transparencies, looking on 6 × 4.5 cm as the smallest acceptable size—a short-sighted view but a commercial fact of life. For this reason, though certainly not as simple to use or carry as a 35 mm camera,

6 × 6 SLRs are greatly favoured by professionals, the Hasselblad being the most popular make.

As a result, some amateurs think that ownership of a Hasselblad outfit will automatically let them turn out work of a professional standard. It won't, any more than purchasing a Formula 1 car will make you a Grand Prix driver—it is just as easy to produce unsaleable results with a Hasselblad as with any other camera.

Hasselblads have become such a standard tool because they are extremely reliable, being hand-built with high precision and with individually tested lenses that are all of a very high standard. Interchangeable magazines let you shoot a lot of films in quick succession (provided you have an assistant to reload for you, rather as the women in a Western reload the guns of the men firing through the windows of a log cabin), all the controls work smoothly and the results will be of the very highest quality.

Snags? All the accessories and lenses are expensive due to the labour involved in manufacture and testing; a basic outfit of a camera with 50, 80 and 150 mm lenses weighs $6\frac{1}{2}$ lb against the $2\frac{1}{2}$ of an Olympus OM–1 with the equivalent 35, 50 and 100 mm lenses; to do justice to the optics and the precision construction it is wise to use a tripod at the slower speeds. In other words it is a very professional instrument that will give superb results in the hands of an experienced photographer who is prepared to trade an increase in weight and bulk over 35 mm equipment in return for an improvement in quality.

The 6 × 6 cm Rollei range is of equally high quality (and price) while Bronica and Mamiya also supply 6 × 6 cm cameras of basically similar design which are less expensive. They all have waist-level finders which give an image reversed left to right (though they can all be fitted with pentaprisms), which is not important since the camera will always be held in the same position for either upright or horizontal compositions.

Many people do in fact prefer waist-level finders, since instead of looking directly at the subject you lower your head to compose the picture on the screen. This brings a feeling of detachment that helps you to concentrate on arranging the picture without being distracted by its surroundings—I know this doesn't sound very logical but it is true.

For very many years the standard 6 × 6 cm camera for professional and advanced amateur use was the twin-lens Rolleiflex, an extremely pleasant and simple instrument to use. There was no flipping mirror or auto diaphragm and since the only thing that moved when you pressed the release was the between lens shutter there was no vibration and surprisingly slow speeds could be used with success. An ideal camera for flash work, it is still used by many pressmen though it was discontinued a long time ago due to the lack of interchangeable lenses. It is now being reintroduced, but at a high price. However, secondhand ones are available, and it should be seriously considered for our purposes.

In order to overcome the fixed-lens problem the Mamiyaflex was introduced, the only twin-lens reflex with interchangeable lenses. Since two of them are mounted on the same panel an outfit is naturally rather heavy and bulky but in my experience the results are excellent. On the whole I would say these cameras are better suited to indoor work, preferably with flash, rather than landscape photography, but they have been used very successfully by some outdoor workers.

Since when making a print from a 6 × 6 cm negative you normally use either a vertical or a horizontal section about 6 × 4.5 cm in size, several cameras have been produced that use this format in order to reduce the size of the camera and to obtain more frames on the roll. However, since the camera has to be turned sideways to take vertical pictures a pentaprism has to be fitted in the same way as on a 35 mm camera, adding to the bulk and weight. In spite of this such cameras are usually still lighter and more compact than the 6 × 6 cm equivalent, and they do produce transparencies saleable to publishers who are prejudiced against 35 mm. They give quality comparable to 6 × 6 cm cameras made to a similar standard, have interchangeable lenses and usually interchangeable magazines and are in many ways like a scaled-up 35 mm reflex.

Most of the 6 × 7 cm and 6 × 9 cm reflexes have "revolving backs" so that both vertical and horizontal pictures can be taken with the camera held in the same position. They are heavy enough to warrant the use of a tripod and can give big, beautiful transparencies and prints of outstanding quality but, like stand cameras, they call for a more planned and slower approach to a subject than is needed with, say, a 35 mm camera. They are not the cameras to take with you on a day's walk over rough country.

Apart from the rangefinder, direct-vision finder versions, nearly all the medium format SLRs have interchangeable magazines but these are not used, as some amateurs imagine, to switch back and forth from colour to black and white. As has been mentioned, their main purpose is to speed up the time lapse between film changes. A professional going on an outdoor assignment knows if the result is needed in colour or black and white and loads accordingly. Our work puts us in a rather different position since, as will be explained later, it is often very useful to bring home pictures of the same subject in both colour and black and white so that the potential buyer has a choice. Interchangeable magazines may seem the answer, but unless the emulsions have exactly the same speed adjustments must be made to metering and either stop or shutter speed at every change. In addition changing magazines takes your mind off the subject and can be time consuming.

If I am using 35 mm therefore, as I do a great deal, I prefer to carry a spare camera body loaded with colour and with the meter set to the correct emulsion speed. I find it much quicker and easier to swap lenses from one body to another than to change magazines. In the days when I used the twin-lens Rollei I found them light and compact enough to carry two, one loaded with colour, the other with black and white, and since there was no question of changing lenses I just got on with taking pictures; there were no operating decisions to be made.

Large Format Cameras

If you are hoping to sell transparencies for use as magazine covers or for calendars showing the beauties of Britain there is no doubt that a colourful 5″ × 4″ of high quality will be much more acceptable and will give better reproduction than a 6 × 6 cm equivalent. For these purposes it is worth considering the use of a large format camera. The outfit will inevitably be large and heavy, especially since a tripod will normally be used, and a planned and methodical approach to the subject is essential.

Once asked to produce large format transparencies of various locations in Epping Forest, I completed the whole job in a morning because I had a guide who knew exactly where to go, a tractor pulling a trailer with a bale of hay on which to sit and place my equipment, and a day for which fine weather had been forcast. The only effort required on my part was to choose the angle and set up the camera.

On the other hand, producing 5″ × 4″ specimens for Polaroid of typical country scenes using a Speed Graphic outfit, I was silly and optimistic enough to plod over the South

Walking along the prehistoric Berkshire Ridgeway at dusk, a flock of starlings flew across on their way to roost. I had a 6 × 6cm Rolleiflex, set to give the correct exposure, hanging round my neck and simply had to press the release, but the light was very flat and when I came to print the negative I had to use the hardest paper, Grade 5, to obtain a print with reasonable contrast. Hard paper always exaggerates grain, especially when you have areas of even tone, and had I been using a 35 mm camera the result might have been unsatisfactory. However I managed to get away with it using the larger negative. If you have to cover any distance on foot you appreciate the fact that a twin-lens Rollei is much lighter and more compact than the average 35 mm outfit, though not of course as versatile.

Keep a look out for the absurdly sentimental statues beloved by the Victorians—pictures of them are very saleable. They are most often found in old cemeteries but these were in the Conservatory at Chiswick House. I had no idea they existed until a gardener I was talking to told me about them. The ever-valuable 24mm lens included the three of them in spite of the cramped space, the depth of field at f8 being quite sufficient while the diffused light gave an almost shadowless result. There's a book waiting to be written on Victorian sculpture; a mass of it has survived throughout the country.

Downs hoping subjects would appear of their own accord—I am only just beginning to walk upright once more! At least it taught me never to go on a photographic expedition without having a number of pre-planned basic locations researched in advance no matter what type of camera I am using.

Successful large format photography calls for considerable experience of the effect of the various camera movements. Given this, you can take architectural pictures in which the uprights do not tilt, the horizontals do not converge and the whole area of the film is filled with the subject. Depth of field can be greatly increased by the use of swings and tilts and you have complete control over perspective. A lens with a maximum aperture of f5.6 is quite large enough, thus saving weight and cost, but your tripod must be large and sturdy.

However, this is a specialised branch of photography more suited to full-time professionals rather than to the weekend amateur. In return for a lot of time and trouble you get the best possible result with static subjects but large format photography demands skill, enthusiasm and a planned approach.

If you decide to record Britain seriously there will always be the temptation to exchange your present camera for one that is more "modern", perhaps taking a different film size. This may well be a retrograde step, since it takes at least a year for an amateur to reach the stage where he handles his camera automatically, without conscious thought. If your present camera gives you satisfactory results it may be wise to keep on using it since familiarity with your apparatus is infinitely more important than its scope.

Amongst the more elementary mistakes I have made was that of going out on an important expedition with an unfamiliar camera that I was assured could tackle any subject more successfully than the ten-year-old SLR I was using—I became so uneasy at finding the controls in different places, and so undecided about which mode to use, that I hardly spared a thought for the subjects and the results were poor. Never, ever use new apparatus for the first time on subjects that matter.

Buying Secondhand

The first thing to remember is that though you won't get a bargain from a dealer you should get peace of mind. Having bought or more likely part-exchanged a camera the dealer will check and test it, making sure it works efficiently and is in reasonable condition. This takes time and money and in addition he has his rent, wages, general overheads and VAT to consider. So though it may appear that he is offering a low price for a camera and selling it for a high one this is almost inevitable, especially if he includes a guarantee.

If you don't mind taking a slight gamble you will probably get better value by buying direct from the owner, especially if he has approached a dealer beforehand and been dismayed at the price he has been offered. The risk is that you may be offered a faulty camera that the dealer has rejected, and so private sales must be treated with caution.

When examining the apparatus, take with you a strong magnifying glass and start by checking the surfaces of the back and front elements of the lens under a glancing light. A network of very fine scratches shows it has been cleaned at some time with a coarse handkerchief and as a result the pictures will be slightly diffused. A single small scratch at the edge of the element or even a small chip out of it may not noticeably affect the results (any danger of scatter can be eliminated by filling it in with matt black paint, using a

Shortly before I was due to give a lecture in Salisbury I wandered down to the river, just as the sun set. There was still a glow in the sky and as mist rose around the Cathedral a girl on a horse rode into just the right position to make a picture. This of course was pure luck, but they were only there for a moment so the camera had to be raised and the picture taken without delay. Unless you are using a fully automatic camera it pays to keep it set on the right exposure and focused not on infinity but at a distance which just includes infinity on the depth of field scale.

Here I was experimenting with the 15 mm Zeiss Hologon, an amazing lens that though suffering from a certain amount of vignetting (a darkening of the corners of the picture) had high contrast and reproduced straight lines correctly. Like all super wides it gave a sense of movement to the clouds in the sky and produced a perspective which though correct seemed startling and exaggerated. In order to obtain the necessary precision the lens was built into its own camera; no focusing was necessary due to the enormous depth of field at its fixed aperture, f8. The angle covered, 110°, was so great that the camera had to be used with a pistol grip in order to keep fingers out of the picture!

spotting brush) but if it occurred because the lens was dropped on a hard surface, indicated by a dent in the rim of the mount, one or more of the elements may have been jolted out of position, spoiling the definition.

Examine also the heads of all the screws. A slight burring over of the slots is the sign of an amateur attempt at repair and the camera is best avoided. Dents or scratches on the body indicate careless handling but may not be otherwise important.

Watch the shutter blinds at slow speeds and see that they are not jerky or hesitant—at high speeds they probably work efficiently. Check also the auto diaphragm to see if the blades close evenly and quickly. Remove the lens and examine the mirror for scratches. Pay particular attention to the metering (don't accept the excuse that "The camera hasn't got a battery in it at the moment" or "I think it's stale") and check the flash circuits, both hot-shoe and plug-in. If the meter is a stop or so out you can probably compensate for this by adjusting the "+ or − exposure setting" dial.

These days even a minor repair or overhaul is expensive and if necessary must be added to the cost of the camera, so careful checking is essential, otherwise you may end up spending far more than if you had bought the same instrument from a dealer. Always expect the worst.

Given all this, it is still possible to obtain a genuine bargain. In the pre-Olympus days, professional 35 mm SLRs and their lenses tended to be large and heavy and are now looked on as old-fashioned. If you can find one—perhaps a 1972 Minolta XE-1, or a Canon F-1 of the same period—that has seen occasional use by an amateur, it will work as well as when new and will produce results of high quality for many years to come. Since most amateurs these days want their cameras to be light, compact and multi-mode you may be able to purchase very professional apparatus at a comparatively low price.

Beware cameras that have been used for a long period by working photographers. They have probably exposed many thousands of films, have had a lively life and be in need of a complete overhaul with the costly renewal of worn parts. Some amateurs change their cameras each spring so as to stay with the latest fashion and such instruments will probably be as new and possibly still under guarantee.

If you wish to gain experience in medium format photography your best bargain will be an amateur-owned twin-lens Rolleiflex. Provided it is in good condition and has a flash-synchronised shutter it will produce within its limitations much higher quality than a 35 mm, and its Compur shutter will let you use flash in daylight at any speed. The least expensive models will have f3.5 Tessar or Xenar lenses. The f3.5 Xenotar costs more but gives better covering power at open aperture, whilst the bigger and heavier Rolleis with f2.8 Planars or Xenotars give outstanding definition but are much in demand and are consequently expensive.

You may be offered a Rollei with an 80 mm f2.8 Tessar. Avoid it—though a collector's item the lens is not up to standard.

Lenses

The standard lens for a 35 mm camera has a focal length of 50 mm and in the case of professional cameras a maximum aperture of f2—ones that are also intended for the amateur market will be f1.8 because beginners tend to think the bigger the aperture the

Using a 100mm lens, a minimum shutter speed of 1/250th was needed even though the action was directly towards the camera but the light was so poor that a stop of f5.6 had to be used, giving little depth of field. It is almost impossible to focus on such a moving object manually (automatic focusing may not be fast enough either) and the answer was to focus sharply on a spot on the ground and to release the shutter as the leading runner reached it. Practice is needed since there is a slight delay between pressing the release and the operation of the shutter, the exact time depending on the make of camera. You need to anticipate the peak of the action.

If you are buying a 17 or 18 mm lens try to get one with built-in filters; ones that fit over the very large front element are expensive and bulky. Here a medium yellow on a 17 mm Tamron was turned into position and darkened the sky satisfactorily while late evening sunshine made a fairly ordinary row of houses seem interesting. I wish the ducks had been swimming into the picture instead of out of it but you can't have everything..... Super wide lenses are invaluable for both landscapes and architectural work and I carry one with me all the time. They give movement to clouds in the sky and produce an eye-catching perspective that makes a conventional subject saleable. Incidentally, this Hampstead pond was constructed by the Elizabethans to supply water to London. I live in one of the houses.

better. Some f1.4 lenses of very high quality are also available but for our particular purposes are probably quite unnecessary and will seldom if ever be used at open aperture.

6 × 6 cm cameras usually have 80 mm f2.8 lenses and the 6 × 4.5 cm format a 75 mm lens of similar or slightly larger aperture. There is little point in having an aperture larger than this since by loading with 400 ASA material instead of 125 ASA you get satisfactory quality from the larger area and nearly two stops increase in speed, an f2.8 becoming the equivalent in terms of exposure of an f1.4 with 125 ASA film.

To get the best from 35 mm you must compose the picture so that the whole of the frame is used, and this means that lenses with a focal length both longer and shorter than normal will have to be used to record the variety of subjects we will encounter, also letting us control the pespective. Interchangeable lenses are less vital, though still desirable, with medium format cameras since the negatives are big enough for just a part of them to be enlarged without much loss in quality.

Lenses for 35 mm SLRs can be divided into two main groups, "straight" ones, also known as "prime" lenses that have a fixed focal length, and "zooms" in which the focal length can be varied while the lens remains in focus on the same point. Professionals tend to prefer straight lenses (though zooms are gradually becoming accepted, especially when used on autofocus cameras) while amateurs use zooms.

The reasons for this are a little complicated. Straight lenses give greater sharpness than most zooms though the latter are rapidly catching up, have bigger maximum apertures giving a brighter screen image which is easy to focus critically, are lighter, more compact and in most cases cheaper.

The sole advantage of the zoom is that the one lens includes a range of focal lengths—one with a range of from 35 to 135 mm, for instance, is equivalent to 35, 50, 75, 100 and 135 mm lenses together with all the settings in between and it seems logical to the amateur to buy just a single lens rather than a range of straight ones. It will cost less, take up less room in the gadget bag and will let you compose a picture tightly without altering your position. Why, you may ask, does anyone still buy straight lenses?

If you have only handled zooms in a dealer's shop the disadvantages are largely hidden. The most popular type includes a range of approximately 75 to 210 mm, all the longer-than-normal focal lengths you are ever likely to need, and if the maximum aperture is f4 the diameter of the stop when wide open will be 50 mm—such a lens will inevitably be fairly large and heavy. If you carry it on a camera hanging from a strap round your neck for long periods it can be both tiring and clumsy. The same thing applies to an even greater extent if you have an outfit consisting of a camera with just a single zoom running from a wide angle of perhaps 28 mm to a long focus of 135 mm, since the weight will be there all the time.

Though the maximum aperture of a zoom is limited this is not very important from the point of view of exposure since emulsions are continually increasing in speed without any lowering of quality. However, at the shorter focal lengths the small maximum aperture may make it difficult to focus and you will find yourself zooming to the longest focal length, focusing and then re-composing the picture—an unwanted distraction. There is also the odd fact that no matter how experienced the photographer there is an almost irresistible temptation to pause after focusing and composing the picture and make a slight alteration to the focal length so as to include slightly more or slightly less of the subject; the delay can cause you to miss the picture.

I'm not keen on zoo photography since I don't like to see animals in cages, but in the Dublin Zoo they seem to have a great deal of freedom and these giraffes made an irresistible subject. To increase the apparent height I used a Rolleiflex from a kneeling position and waited patiently until these dignified creatures turned their heads in the same direction towards an approaching keeper. You can't rush animal photography; very occasionally you get a good picture at once but usually you have to wait a long time for them to get into the right position.

There is no harbour at Hastings and the fishing boats have to charge the pebble beach at high tide to get as high up as possible before a cable is attached to winch them up. By checking the tide tables you can find the right time to be there and then it's just a case of finding an appropriate foreground. A 135 mm lens compressed the perspective and since the movement was towards the camera a medium stop and a comparatively slow shutter speed (1/250th) could be used.

On the other hand zooms are great fun to use and consequently have a universal appeal to the hobby-photographer, but often all common sense seems to be lost when buying one. If, for instance, you were buying a set of straight lenses, would you include a 300 or even a 200 mm in your outfit? How often would you need such a long focal length unless you were specialising in sports or press photography? Yet most amateurs carry zooms that include long focal lengths that will never be used, adding to the bulk and weight and making it necessary to buy large, expensive filters. For our kind of work a focal length longer than 135 mm will hardly ever be needed and a 70—150 mm zoom will cover all our requirements.

The difficulty for the inexperienced worker is that when setting out for a day's photography he has no idea what lenses will be needed and consequently carries enough equipment to cope with every possible eventuality, no matter how unlikely. Once in a thousand subjects he will come across a scene that would be best taken by, say, a 300 mm lens but carrying heavy equipment all the time quickly kills the enthusiasm that is necessary for successful photography. It's much better to miss the odd picture in return for handling the majority happily.

The most common straight lens outfit is a 28, a 50 and a 135 mm lens but in my experience most people and places can be more successfully taken with a 24 mm wide angle (half the focal length of the normal lens), a 50 mm (which since it will have a large maximum aperture will be invaluable in poor light) and a 100 mm (twice the normal focal length). In addition I always carry a 17 mm super-wide for use in tight corners or for occasions when I want to take unusual—and saleable—pictures of hackneyed subjects. Unlike fisheye lenses, it reproduces straight lines correctly and covers the whole frame.

Any of these lenses can be carried on the camera for long periods without discomfort and have both high definition and good covering power even at full aperture, which is not always true of zooms. In order to fill the frame it is necessary to physically adjust the distance between the camera and the subject instead of standing on one spot and zooming back and forth and on occasion this can be difficult, but I feel the advantages of straight lenses outweigh the disadvantages. Other photographers may feel exactly the opposite since techniques and subject matter vary so greatly.

There is a lot to be said for buying a set of lenses made by the manufacturer of your camera since stops and focusing will all turn in the same direction and they will probably all take the same size of filter, saving money and space. Lenses made by independent companies can be of a very high standard and may well be cheaper than similar ones supplied by the camera maker but they may be more inconvenient to use.

"Bargain" lenses are unsuitable for serious work since the standard of inspection will have been low with optically inferior lenses not being weeded out, the focusing may soon stiffen up or develop backlash, the diaphragm may become inaccurate, especially at small stops, and the lens mount may have been made from soft metal that will wear quickly. The price of lenses made by firms such as Leitz reflects the fact that every lens is as near optical perfection as possible and the mechanical functions will be as smooth and accurate in fifty years time as they are now. Money spent on obtaining really good lenses is never wasted.

Medium Format Lenses

The standard set of lenses for a 6 × 6 cm SLR consists of a 50, an 80 and a 150 mm, equivalent to a 35, 50 and 100 mm on a 35 mm camera. Zoom lenses are large, expensive and very rare since it is difficult to compute one to cover such a large area of film and they are hardly ever needed by the kind of photographer who uses this format. The 50 and the 150 will probably have a maximum aperture of around f4 in order to reduce the size and weight.

For true long focus work lenses of around 250 mm are available but the average photographer will find the standard set quite enough to carry for any distance. I admit to an obsession with the bulk and weight of equipment, an obsession you will share after you have clambered up and down hills and walked for some miles over rough country looking for pictures.

Lenshoods

One of the many photographic myths is that a lenshood is unnecessary with a coated lens. Modern coating has done a great deal to eliminate scatter from lens elements but all lenses include more of the subject than is needed for the picture. Unwanted light from this surrounding area can be reflected from the internal walls of the camera and lens barrel, even though they have been blackened, onto the emulsion to cause a slight flattening of the image and a consequent reduction in the apparent sharpness of the picture.

To be efficient a hood should be large, extending well forward in the case of long focus lenses. For work in the field it should be made of metal or strong plastic and be rigid, not collapsible. There are two reasons for this: in the first place it will protect the front elements against knocks and damage and in the second the lens can be stored in the gadget bag hood down with just the back cap in place, ready for fast lens changing. Screw-on or bayonet-fitting hoods are more likely to stay in place than the push-on types.

Hoods on super-wide lenses do little to reduce unwanted light but since the front elements of these lenses usually curve well forward they have an important protective function.

Filters

Black and white landscapes intended for reproduction in books and magazines should have bold, obvious skys; subtle cloud formations against a light grey sky may be suitable for exhibitions but will not catch the eye of either the picture editor or the reader.

For this reason an orange filter will be used more than any other. It will in addition bring out detail in brick or stone buildings and in woodwork, and though some landscape workers carry in addition a green filter to lighten leaves and grass I carry just the orange for the sake of simplicity.

For colour work most editors prefer warm, definite colours and the blue haze that occurs in distant landscapes and the cold cast of pictures taken on overcast days or in the shade must be avoided. Haze, often invisible to the eye, records on film due to the ultra-violet light that is present. Modern lenses filter out quite a lot of this automatically and very weak, almost colourless "Haze" or U.V. filters will only have a very slight effect, their main use being to protect the front element of the lens. Haze filters are often supplied in different strengths and the most effective will show a pale straw colour when placed on a

Doing some publicity work at Hever Castle in Kent I was using the amazing 15mm Hologon lens. The weather started to cloud over (the forecast in Britain is rarely 100% reliable, which adds to the interest of outdoor photography) so landscapes were abandoned and I retired to the Italian Garden. The bust was some two feet away from the lens, the archway perhaps six—using a lens with such a wide angle the perspective becomes wildly exaggerated. Though the camera was loaded with 400 ASA film, at the fixed stop of f8 it had become so dark that a shutter speed of 1/30th was needed. However there was no danger of camera shake since 1/30th with a 15mm lens is equivalent in terms of movement to 1/100th with a 50mm.

If you are buying a super wide, check that straight lines remain straight in the photograph. Some of the earlier lenses of this type had bad barrel distortion which makes architectural work impossible—beware of ones offered at bargain prices.

sheet of white paper. Skylight filters are pale amber in colour and can be left permanently on the lens when working in dull, overcast weather.

Since a skylight filter also cuts through haze I tend to carry just this filter for colour work, even though distant landscapes can appear over-warm. Anything I can do to simplify equipment is well worth while.

Amateurs sometimes use "effect" filters which give vignetted, diffused, multi-image or star-burst effects but the pictures they produce do not sell. Unless specifically requested, stick to the straight-forward photography that most editors require.

"Graduated" filters, clear at the bottom and coloured at the top, have their uses in producing dramatic skies without affecting the foreground but they must be used with great discretion, the very pale tobacco-coloured ones probably being most useful. When using one, press the "stop-down" or "pre-view" button before taking the picture so that you can see what the effect will be at the working stop—it varies according to the aperture.

When working in the late evening the low sunlight gives a decidedly orange cast to the scene and some workers use a blue filter to overcome this effect. If you do this (and I doubt if it is worthwhile) use only the palest blue since any attempt to match noon daylight gives a very odd look to the transparency. One expects a landscape with very long shadows to have a warm coloration and if it has the neutral appearance given by midday sunlight it appears completely unnatural.

The only way in which you can darken skys when using colour film is to use a polarising filter. This cuts out some of the light scattered by the atmosphere (this is why the higher you fly the deeper blue becomes the sky), the effect being greatest when the camera is pointing at right angles to the position of the sun, that is to say towards the South in the morning or evening when the sun is in the East or West; at midday when the sun is in the South the camera should point East or West. The filter has little effect when the sun is behind the camera or when you are shooting into the light.

It has other important effects in landscape work besides simply darkening the sky. Since it cuts out some of the scatter it penetrates haze in the distance, giving clearer results with greater colour saturation. It also reduces reflections from shiny surfaces such as leaves, grass, corn and flowers, giving much more brilliant colouring—sometimes the effect is almost unnatural, the scene looking as though it had been painted with flat poster paint. Not all landscapes are improved by the use of a polarising filter.

It can be very useful on days with overcast skys, common in Britain, greatly improving colour saturation by cutting out the reflections caused by diffused and scattered white light and producing results almost as brightly coloured as those taken on sunny days.

Polarising filters are best used on SLRs. They are usually fitted in a rotating mount, the image being viewed on the screen and the filter turned until the effect is at its greatest; if you have a camera with a direct vision viewfinder you have to look at the scene through the filter, turn it and then fit it to the lens hoping you have kept it in the same position. The filter factor will be around ×3, depending on the make. This will be taken care of by your through-the-lens metering.

If streams or rivers have been included in your picture the filter can greatly reduce reflections from the surface of the water, sometimes letting you see the pebbles on the bottom. Once again, this can appear unnatural and if in doubt take two pictures, one with the filter and one without.

Every rail passenger to Brighton crosses the Ouse valley by means of this long brick viaduct at Balcombe but not many people see if from the valley floor. If they did they would find each support has a hole in the middle and by standing at one end you can look right through the entire length of the viaduct—it's a very odd effect. A small stop gave the necessary depth of field and an overcast day gave even lighting. The old bucket which provides a centre of interest just happened to be there, honestly.

The skulls in the Parish Church of Hythe, Kent, are dimly lit but I felt that flash would kill the atmosphere. Using 400 ASA film the exposure needed was $\frac{1}{2}$ a second at f2.8, so I set the 17 mm Tamron lens to open aperture and used a monopod. The angle was so wide that the custodian had no idea he was being included in the picture. This is one of the useful aspects of a super wide lens—anyone near the edges of the field remains quite unselfconscious.

Flash

For the novice who is taking up serious flash photography for the first time there is always the temptation to buy one of the big, heavy, professional outfits, forgetting that it will sometimes have to be carried all day. They look impressive and their power capacity can be vital on occasion but only if you are going to specialise in flash work. For our kind of photography a small, light unit which fits in a gadget bag pocket is far more practical, and even then it should only be carried if you think you will use it.

To produce interesting and saleable pictures an extension lead is essential. There are occasions—if you are in a crowd for instance—when the flash will have to be used on the camera but this gives flat "press photographer" lighting. For most of our pictures we will have the time and space to hold the camera in one hand and the flash at arm's length in the other, giving some shape and modelling to the subject. You might think that operating the camera with a single hand would lead to shake but the flash duration is so brief, probably 1/1000th of a second, that it cannot occur provided you are working indoors in subdued light.

There are three ways of obtaining correct exposure. The traditional method is to use the guide number supplied by the manufacturer with every unit for use when the flash is set on "Manual". Let's say you are photographing a carved benchend in a church; the carving is four feet from the flash, the church walls perhaps sixty feet and you want the subject to stand out against a black background. The guide number of the unit with the film you are using is 80 so you divide 4 into 80 and set the stop at the result, f22 being close enough. However, the manufacturers presume you will be taking your picture in a normal living room with light walls and ceiling to reflect extra light towards the subject. This is not the case in a large church and the lens will have to be opened an extra stop, to f16. This system has the advantage that the photographer decides for himself which part of the scene he wants to be correctly exposed. In addition, since he is using the full power of the flash he is also using the smallest possible stop, obtaining maximum depth of field. After experience has been gained the guide number is little used—you know instinctively what stop is needed.

The second and by far the most common system is to use an "automatic" or "computerised" flash in which the light reflected back from the subject falls on a sensor which cuts off the flash when enough light has reached the film to give the correct exposure. With normal subjects this works well but going back to our benchend, if we are working with a long focus lens the sensor, which has a fixed angle of acceptance, may include too much of the surrounding dark church and will try to compromise, over-exposing the bench. the same thing can happen if the main object is to one side of the frame.

The most modern system uses "through-the-lens flash metering", a sensor inside the camera measuring the light reflected from the area included by the lens whatever its focal length. Some also take into consideration the existing ("ambient") light and automatically give you the correct balance between flash and daylight. A flash unit specially designed to suit the camera must be used, and is usually fairly expensive.

As a power source, rechargeable batteries are preferable to disposable ones since the day before you set off on an expedition you can charge them to capacity. With disposable batteries there is always the temptation to take a chance on part-used ones lasting out the day and you can be sure they will lose power, causing a very long recycling time, just when

Though it is best to work with the natural existing light if possible, flash is often essential. Three units were used for this picture of a potter, two lighting the far corner and the shelves and one from the right lighting the subject. A 35mm lens was needed to include the whole of the scene, the stop being f22 on FP4 with three Courtenay Sola 2 units at full power. These have modelling lights which cut out the guesswork when positioning them and, more important, have never given the slightest trouble in spite of having been carried all over the British Isles in the boot of a car. For professional work reliability is much more important than versatility.

you need them most.

If you take all the advertisements seriously it is easy to get to the state where you feel you cannot take flash pictures unless you use the very latest technical developments. This is not so; they are a convenience but you can obtain equally successful results with the most basic flash and a little thought.

Multi-Flash

If you are going to specialise in flash work there is a great deal to be said for buying two or more units. Unless you are trying to photograph large areas the smaller types will be perfectly suitable, but of course you have to find a way of firing them all at the same moment. This can be done by connecting leads—wires that link the triggering circuits of the units together—but it is much more convenient to use inexpensive "slave units" that plug into the flash contacts and close the circuits instantaneously when struck by a pulse of light.

One flash is connected directly to the camera and fires the rest. Some workers like to place the extra units on stands or tripods or have them held by assistants but the travelling photographer will probably position them by using small clamps that can be fixed to furniture, pipes, shelves, etc.

Theoretically, all the units should be set on manual and used at full power but I have had good results using automatic flashes, varying their output to obtain interesting lighting. This is not the place to discuss lighting arrangements since there are many good books on the subject, but it is best to place the units well apart so that they cover the area evenly but at the same time give modelling.

Flash In Daylight

The older type of focal plane shutter that synchronises with flash at a single speed, perhaps 1/60th, is difficult to use for "synchro-sunlight" photography, that is using the flash to fill in harsh shadows out of doors. Having set the shutter you then have to choose a stop that will give correct exposure for the sunlit parts of the subject, which when using 125 ASA material could be either f16 or f22, but to have much effect at this small stop the flash must be either very close to the subject or else very powerful.

The more modern 35mm SLRs often have shutters that synchronise at 1/125th or even 1/250th, making the use of flash in daylight much more simple, but easiest of all to use are cameras with between lens shutters that synchronise at any speed. This is why so many pressmen still use ancient twin-lens Rolleis while advertising and fashion workers use Hasselblads.

There are many ways of obtaining the correct balance and exposure when using these cameras for synchro-sunlight photography, some so complicated you'd need a calculator to work them out. The system I use is, as you would expect, very simple to grasp and operate. Setting the flash on manual you estimate the distance to the subject, divide it into the guide number and set the stop accordingly, just as though you were taking a picture indoors. Let's say the answer is f8. You then set the shutter at whatever speed will give the correct exposure to the sunlit areas, perhaps 1/250th. If you take the picture at this combination the effect of the flash will be fairly obvious with plenty of light in the

A major advantage of cameras with waist-level finders is that it is a simple matter to take pictures from ground level. Photographing a cobbled street from a standing position with the camera held to the eye will result in a conventional picture, but here working in Rye with a Rollei I could almost rest it on the stones; strong backlighting helped to produce the effect of a sea of cobbles. It's surprising what an important part the small figure plays.

Photographing the British Museum from the entrance gate with a standard lens simply results in a boring picture of part of the central portico; the useful 17 mm Tamron produces a more eye-catching picture. The built-in yellow filter was turned into position to darken the sky, the pillars were lined up with the edges of the screen to make sure the camera was properly upright and a porter was included to give a feeling of depth. I normally carry 17, 24, 50 and 100 mm lenses and look on the 17 mm as being at least as essential as the others; if I were limited to just a couple of lenses I'd choose the 17 and the 100 mm. Incidentally you are free to take pictures, even with flash, in the Museum, and in summer the tourists are even more strange and photographable than the exhibits. Tripods are of course forbidden but provided you can work at f2.8 or a larger aperture you should be able to use shutter speeds that let you hand hold the camera in most areas provided you use 400 ASA or faster film.

shadow areas, but we must remember that outdoors the power of the flash is almost halved due to the lack of reflecting surfaces, so the effect is not as marked as you might expect.

This is the technique I would use to photograph someone standing in heavy shade under a tree in a sunny landscape. For more subtle results I would close the lens down by one stop to f11 and slow the shutter down to 1/125th; this would help to preserve the natural effect of the daylight.

Hi-tech cameras are now available that obtain a pleasing balance between flash and daylight automatically. Set on "program" they select a combination of stop and shutter speed for you and adjust the power of the flash to the correct brightness. Things become so easy that there is a danger of the user becoming a flash-addict, using it for every picture. The results become monotonous and don't sell.

Bounce Flash

Soft, even lighting over a big area can be obtained by bouncing the light from the ceiling or walls instead of pointing it directly towards the subject. The power of the light is considerably reduced, an increase of perhaps three stops in exposure being needed compared to direct flash, depending on the size of the room and the lightness of the walls.

Though once again with experience you can guess the stop needed with surprising accuracy, this is a situation where an automatic flash or a camera with through-the-lens flash metering is invaluable since it makes guessing or measuring unnecessary. It must be possible to tilt the flash head and preferably swivel it to the side as well, the body with its sensor remaining pointing towards the subject.

The standard technique is to bounce the light from the ceiling, tilting the head into the vertical position for horizontal pictures and swivelling it when taking upright ones so that the flash falls on the same area. The results are often over-flat and characterless, especially when using black and white, and since the light falls on people's heads from above, the eye sockets tend to be in shadow, giving a sad-looking picture.

Much more interesting lighting is obtained by pointing the flash towards the angle where the wall meets the ceiling or even at the wall behind you or to one side, always keeping the sensor pointing towards the subject. For units with a limited amount of swivel and tilt, "remote sensors" are sometimes available which connect to the flash by an extension lead. If you are specialising in interiors it is worth using two flashes, a powerful unit to give soft all-over bounce lighting while a smaller direct one gives some shape and modelling.

However, for 90% of our flash photography a small, light unit with an extension lead will do everything we need. It will take time to learn how to use it to best advantage but this is inevitable and part of our photographic education. Don't always rely on advanced electronics to do the thinking for you; you can't improve on your own taste and judgement.

Carrying Your Equipment

At one time all serious photographers carried their equipment in an oblong case made from strong plywood covered with solid hide. It gave complete protection, lasted forever and was so strong that you could use it as a seat while waiting for an event to take place.

The problem was to show the winding track of the East Sussex Railway as it approached Tenterden. Railway curves are really quite gentle so a 135 mm lens was used to compress the distance and make the bends seem sharper. Since the movement was towards the camera and the train was chugging slowly up the steep gradient there was no need to use a high shutter speed and a small enough stop could be set to obtain good depth of field.

The disadvantages were the weight, cost and the fact that it was uncomfortable to carry for any distance, banging against your side if you moved quickly while the sharp corners made you unpopular in crowds.

As a result some 35 mm camera owners started using fishing bags or ex-Army haversacks instead, which had the added advantage that the user could not be immediately identified as a professional photographer. These developed into the very popular "soft bags" which are a boon to photographers who have to carry their equipment for long distances or for long periods.

The advantages are that to a certain extent it moulds itself to your side and does not bang against you as you walk, it is comparatively light and in many cases will expand to take extra equipment. Though it does not give quite the same protection as the older hard cases the contents are usually cushioned by padding.

Unfortunately there are many cheap, poorly made bags about which will not stand up to the kind of treatment they will encounter at the hands of the travelling photographer. In my experience the base of the bag should be stiff, perhaps made from a sheet of foam-covered plywood, the zips should be of the heavy-duty variety, not the domestic kind, and should follow gentle curves rather than go round sharp right angles, and the carrying strap should be some 2" wide and made from a fairly stiff material such as webbing which will not fold or crease. Velcro "Touch fastenings" on the lids and pockets work well to start with but soon become clogged with dust and fibres and lose their grip unless they are cleaned constantly—I prefer the old-fashioned brass stud pushed through a slit in a leather strap. It will be stiff at first but will soon work smoothly with use.

It is easy to make the mistake of buying a bag that just holds your outfit with no spare room. When changing lenses there must be an empty compartment into which you can place the lens you have removed before you fit the new one, otherwise you will find yourself with a lens in each hand; it is always better to carry a bag that is larger than you strictly need.

Like so many other professionals I have used Billingham bags since they first appeared. They are in some ways "old-fashioned", being made from very strong waterproof material with solid hide reinforcements and straps, brass studs and buckles, and consequently they have a weight which is greater than many equivalent types but they do stand up to the unavoidably rough treatment they receive. In one day I might carry one through heavy rain, stand it in a puddle on a gravestone, plonk it down in a muddy field, carry it through a barbed wire fence and get it splashed by salt spray, but it never seems to be affected so I feel the extra weight is justified.

Getting ready for an expedition I might pack a nylon raincoat, a map of the area I am covering and any other paperwork in the large, flat back pocket. In the six padded compartments of the main body is a 35 mm SLR with a 50 mm lens, an extra body loaded with colour, a long focus lens, a wide angle one and a super-wide 17 mm, all stowed lenshoods down with the backcaps in place, leaving one empty space for lens-changing. In the next section of the bag I carry filters, a spare camera battery and if the work calls for it, a small flashgun with an extension lead. Finally, one of the two outer pockets is full of unexposed film while the other is empty, ready to receive the exposed cassettes.

Nothing is carried that will not be used during the course of the day. There is no point in taking extra-long focus lenses, bellows units, all your filters and so on just because you feel it is possible you might need them. Keep your outfit as simple as you can and take

When working in black and white an orange filter will be most useful if photographing landscapes and buildings for publication. It will of course make clouds stand out boldly against a dark sky but it also brings life and contrast to stone and brick. The rose-coloured Herstmonceux Castle, a brick-built transition between the mediaeval fort and the manor house, calls out for an orange filter; with no filter the bricks appear flat and monotonous. Most photographers quite rightly think that framing a scene with branches is corny, but the public doesn't and editors try to give them what they want.

your pictures with what you've got.

A large foam-rubber shoulder pad prevents the carrying strap from either cutting into or slipping off my shoulder. The bag is normally slung from my left shoulder since it is easy to slip it off and place it on the ground, but if clambering over rough country it is sometimes safer to place the strap round your neck so that it rests on your right shoulder in the same way that a soldier carries a haversack, the bag being swivelled round in front of you when you need to get at the contents.

The owners of the more expensive medium format outfits, who will probably not want to carry them very far, generally prefer to store them in a "hard case" which gives maximum protection. Some use aluminium types, the better ones being water, dust and heat proof, but carrying them is like carrying a suitcase. They also advertise the fact that they hold valuable contents and consequently have to be watched continually. The cheapest ones, sometimes bought by amateurs who want to appear professional, offer little protection and do not last very long.

Camera bags, or single cameras, are best carried in the car by placing the carrying strap round the headrestand adjusting its length so that the base just touches the seat. This will give minimum vibration and prevents the bag or camera from swinging on bends. If you place anything loosely on the seat it may shoot forward on to the floor under hard braking.

The glove compartment is the most vibration-prone part of the car and cameras carried in it may suffer from loosened screws and lens elements. The shelf between the rear seat and the rear window is the hottest area when parked in the sun and films left there will be roasted.

Never leave equipment where it can be seen. If you have to leave it in the car, perhaps while you have a meal, lock it in the boot and then back the car up against a wall or fence so that a potential thief cannot reach it and force it open.

Camera Supports

It is a sad fact that there is no such thing as the perfect tripod for the photographer who has to carry it. If sturdy and heavy enough to avoid vibration it will stop you from walking very far; if light, compact and portable it will probably be of little use. My own solution is to carry a heavy one in the car but to use it only if the subject is within reasonable distance of the parking place. For all other occasions when I need to steady the camera I use a monopod or a convenient wall or tree.

Vibration is most likely to occur with a tripod when the centre pillar is extended, so the greater the height reached by the legs the better. Avoid soft rubber feet—you might as well stand the tripod on three jellies—using hard rubber or plastic ones instead if the metal spike feet could cause damage to the flooring. Use the metal feet whenever possible since they reduce shake considerably.

Most modern tripods have "pan and tilt" heads since they can be sold for use with cine and video cameras as well as with still ones. In order to obtain a smooth panning action many have a long operating handle which is a very considerable inconvenience to the still camera user. The ones that have very short handles are much better suited to our use, but I much prefer a really large "ball and socket" head, one meant for medium or large format cameras—the small ones will not support a 35 mm camera with a long, heavy lens.

I find the ball and socket head much faster and easier to adjust than the pan and tilt

Here I was trying to show the relaxed, informal atmosphere of the restored Kent and East Sussex Railway. The amateur railwaymen chatted while the 1876 "Sutton" stopped to let level crossing gates open and I took the picture with a 105 mm Super Takumar on a Pentax, giving 1/250th at f5.6. Of course I wasn't there by chance; I knew in advance that the train would stop at this particular spot but couldn't of course predict the position of the men—photography is a combination of planning and luck.

variety. Since it swivels in all directions it does not matter if the tripod feet are on uneven ground—a single movement sets the camera correctly both horizontally and vertically. But always remember, the bigger the head the better.

Because I like to get as far away from the car park as possible I find a monopod more generally useful, provided the leg has a good diameter (the thin ones wobble) and the head can be tilted at right angles so that upright pictures can be taken. The fewer sections the leg has the better, but it should extend sufficiently for you to use the camera at eye level without crouching and at the same time be short enough when collapsed to be carried in the gadget bag (mine sticks out a little but this is no inconvenience).

A monopod makes it possible to use shutter speeds that would inevitably cause the camera to shake if handheld—1/8th of a second is usually safe with a 50 mm lens though I would be happier using 1/30th. With long focus lenses it is invaluable since the amount of camera shake is in proportion to the focal length; if you can handhold a 50 mm lens steadily at 1/125th, a 100 mm lens will need 1/250th and a 200 mm one 1/500th to obtain the same degree of sharpness. The opposite is true with wide angles, a 24 mm lens being safe at 1/60th. However, if you use a monopod you can reduce these speeds drastically.

Other camera supports such as "shoulder pods" and "table-top tripods" are more specialised and not so suitable for the general-purpose photography we will be doing. Of course with luck we may find a low stone wall, a stout fence post or some similar steady support for our camera in just the right place, making a tripod or monopod unnecessary, but you can't depend on it. If they are going to sell, your pictures must be dead sharp and failure to use some kind of support in poor light or when using long focus lenses often results in otherwise excellent results being rejected.

Clothing

You may feel that the kind of clothing you wear is unimportant, but it isn't. You will have to carry equipment for long periods over sometimes difficult country and in even the mildest weather will become hot and sweaty, so shirts and underwear should be made from wool or cotton, not from man-made fibres. Socks should be a wool and nylon mix, clothing should be loose (tight jeans are hopeless) and it is worth remembering that completely waterproof jackets are often also airtight.

Boots are often preferable to shoes since they keep out grit, mud and water from wet grass and deep puddles but in summer, shoes—cooler and lighter—may be preferable. I carry a pair of rubber boots (half-Wellingtons) in the car all the time, ready to change into on arrival at a muddy location. Whatever your type of footwear it should have really thick soles, otherwise you will feel every pebble on the path and every crack in the pavement.

Some fashion and advertising photographers deliberately wear flamboyant clothing in order to attract attention to themselves; they want to be noticed and remembered because it may help them to get more work. People trying to record Britain are in quite a different boat—ideally both they and their camera should be invisible and their clothing should be regarded as a form of protective coloration.

Common sense is needed; a floral shirt that would go unnoticed on the beach at Bournemouth might be regarded as outlandish in the Highlands while the field jacket that would be ordinary wear on a Suffolk farm would be out of place in the City. Try to merge into the surroundings.

In the country there is a great deal to be said for some kind of ex-Army field jacket since it has large pockets (provided they are completely free from fluff they can be used to hold lenses), stands up to rough wear and is reasonably waterproof. In very cold weather a couple of light pullovers are warmer than a single heavy one. In showery or stormy weather a nylon waterproof (ordinary plastic tears) is light to carry and gives better protection than a jacket as you make for cover.

"Photographer's Waistcoats" with more than enough pockets to hold all your equipment have advantages and disadvantages. When empty or with just a few items of equipment in the pockets they are light, cool and practical but when fully loaded they become as heavy as a gadget bag but cannot be placed on the ground to give you a rest; the weight is there all the time. They also make you look conspicuous and mark you out as a photographer, which is not a good idea.

On the whole it is best to wear ordinary clothing in which you feel comfortable, carrying equipment in a khaki gadget bag, not a brightly-coloured one. Amateur photography is one of those hobbies that encourages role-playing, with otherwise sane people dressing in a way that they imagine will make them look "professional", but to take successful pictures your whole attention should be concentrated on the subject, not on the effect of your appearance on the public. Do I sound sour? I've just been watching the pupils of a school of photography out on an imaginary assignment....

Which Film?

In order to sell, black and white prints must be sharp, grainfree and with a full range of tones; choosing the right film is the first step in achieving this end. It is always unwise to recommend any particular emulsion in a book, since the speed of technical progress is increasing and a film that has been standard for years may become obsolete overnight. However, it is safe to say that a "medium speed" film, one with a speed of 100 or 125 ASA, is a suitable choice for outdoor work in good weather.

For very many years most people have used either Ilford's FP4 or Kodak's Plus-X under these conditions since the speed of 125 ASA lets you take most subjects with a shutter speed of, say, 1/250th and a stop around f8 or f11, eliminating camera shake and giving good depth of field. With normal development, × 12 enlargements that are grainfree and which show good detail should be possible.

Some workers who only tackled static subjects and who were prepared to use a camera support preferred the higher quality given by the "slow" emulsions with a speed between 25 and 40 ASA. These produced prints with a sharpness very similar to that from medium format cameras but were too slow for general purpose photography. At all times it was worth carrying a few cassettes of "fast" 400 ASA film, HP5 or Tri-X, for use in low-light situations or for action work on dull days, but they were not suitable for landscapes, showing grain on broad, smooth areas such as clouds.

All this has now changed thanks to the introduction of flat-grain ("T-grain") technology, first incorporated in colour negative emulsions. It is now possible to obtain 100 ASA films that have the fine grain and high definition of the previous slow emulsions and 400 ASA ones with the quality of the previous 125 ASA material.

The temptation is to load with the new 400 ASA film and use it for every situation, but it is still wise to use the medium speed, flat-grain 100 ASA film for outdoor work if possible since the increase in the quality of the prints obtained from it is very high. If, however, you are likely to include all kinds of different subjects from open landscapes to pub interiors on the same roll of film, then the new 400 ASA type is the obvious choice.

Whatever make of emulsion you choose, stay with it. When you are starting photography you will probably want to experiment with many different makes and speeds of film. However, once past this stage it is very important to use just one as much as possible until you know the effect of under and over exposure, what happens when you vary the development time, the way in which tones are reproduced and so on. If you chop and

Bateman's, Kipling's former home near Burwash in Sussex, belongs to the National Trust and is consequently photographed many thousands of times each year. A conventional record of it would be hard to sell so instead I tried to convey something of the atmosphere of the author's Sussex stories, concentrating on the fence and footpath leading into the picture and framing the house in the background with the ancient tree. The absence of visitors is due to the fact that I was there well before opening time. The donkey? Just photographer's luck. When I came to print the negative the footpath was not very obvious so I "held it back" with the shadow of one finger to lighten it.

change emulsions you will never learn how to handle any particular one and your work will suffer. Just as you must know your camera intimately, so you must be completely at home with your film.

Colour

At present colour prints are rarely used for reproduction (though much research is being done to make it usable), so from the commercial point of view colour negative material can be ignored. Reversal films that produce transparencies are the only ones to be considered.

Many types are available and these days most of them are good, but they vary in contrast, colour saturation and colour balance—not a lot but enough to be noticeable. As with black and white it is essential to standardise on one film as far as possible, not just to become accustomed to its characteristics but so that all your transparencies will have similar qualities—a collection of slides in which some are too blue, some too green and some over-warm will have little appeal to an editor.

Two basic types are available, those that can be processed at home or in a laboratory within a few hours by the E6 process, and Kodachrome which has to be sent or taken to Kodak with a consequent processing delay. 35 mm Kodachrome comes with speeds of 25, 64 and 200 ASA while E6 films can have speeds up to 3,200 ASA, the 100 ASA variety being most generally useful for our kind of work.

However, I have standardised on Kodachrome 64 when taking pictures that are not urgently required, for two reasons. In the first place it gives superior sharpness, very fine grain and the kind of warm, saturated colours that sell. In the second place the dyes last for a very much longer period without changing or fading than those in the average E6 film, important if you have photographed the kind of subject that will be in demand over and over again for years. In poor light I use 200 ASA Kodachrome so that the colour balance and general appearance will match my other transparencies, the grain being similar to that of E6 films of the same speed.

E6 films can be home-processed and there is a considerable feeling of achievement when you hang up a perfectly exposed, perfectly processed colour film but it calls for time, precision and some form of very accurate temperature control. In addition, unless you are developing a number of films within a short space of time the chemicals may become stale, and of course you have to cut up and mount the frames yourself.

In spite of this many photographers who have had unfortunate experiences at the hands of careless processing laboratories may feel home-processing is worth the effort. I have had valuable films scratched, torn, splashed with chemicals, over and under developed and generally maltreated by the cheap labour some of the smaller establishments employ and if you do find a careful, reliable firm, even if they charge more, stick with them.

Kodachromes are normally returned in plastic or card mounts for easy handling and, if necessary, projection. For commercial purposes, however, card mounts are better since they take pen or pencil. If sending E6 films to a processor it may be necessary to ask for the frames to be mounted, paying extra.

Roll films are cut into strips of three, four, five or six frames depending on the format and are returned in plastic sleeves; you have to cut them into individual frames and place each in a transparent envelope (see chapter on presentation).

The best advice I can give on choosing colour material is very basic: settle on a well-known make of medium speed material, not least because if you run out of film on location you can buy the same make in most places. Don't chop and change, never use faster film than the subject requires and if using E6 try to find a processing laboratory favoured by professionals. And it's worth mentioning that while some editors reject 35 mm transparencies taken on some makes of E6 film automatically, I've never yet met one who won't accept a good Kodachrome.

Many beginners make the mistake of rushing about in all directions looking for pictures; it's much better to let the pictures come to you. Find a good location and wait. It's a very relaxing (lazy if you like) way of producing the results. It's always worth spending half an hour or so on a bridge over a busy river for instance, just to see what will turn up. If you are using a zoom don't try to zoom and focus at the same time. Set the focal length first—perhaps at 135 mm depending on the height of the bridge—and let the subject come into focus. Shutter speeds do not have to be very high since the subject is moving towards the camera.

Planning an Expedition

There are few more pleasant ways of spending a day than to drive through the lanes and back roads of Britain with a camera, hoping that pictures will appear but not worrying too much if they don't. I've done it myself many times, deliberately getting lost, exploring "No Through Way" roads, visiting remote inns and generally enjoying myself. Unfortunately this is sheer self-indulgence that is unlikely to produce any saleable pictures.

I know it sounds very unromantic but if you hope to show a profit on photographing Britain you have to first of all work out how much you are going to spend on a day's photography. Let's say petrol, food and film cost £25; to this you must add a proportion of the cost of actually owning the car and the photographic equipment, and your personal overheads. To simply cover all this you have to take photographs that will sell for perhaps £30 or £40 before you start to make a profit. And you can't do this without careful planning.

I once met a man who had taken a 5″ × 4″ Linhof with a mass of Ektachrome to Ireland, expecting to take enough pictures to more than pay for his holiday. He had never visited the country before, knew nothing about it and just drove about aimlessly waiting for the subjects he had seen on the Irish Tourist Board posters to appear—they didn't. He returned without having exposed a single sheet of film, mumbling about the weather. I felt sorry for him because it could happen to anyone setting off on an expedition, even for an afternoon in the local countryside, without planning or research.

It is impossible to overstress the importance of research before you start photography. Unless you read as much as you can about the area you are going to visit, study maps, look at existing pictures and wade through old guide books you cannot draw up a list of possible subjects in the right order. You will miss all kinds of curiosities, the kind of things that sell so well, ignore ordinary-looking subjects that have an interesting history or connection, miss odd ceremonies and events and simply photograph hackneyed subjects that are over-familiar to every editor.

The weather in this country is what is laughingly called "variable" and at any time of the year you will get a few days when the clouds come right down to the ground and the drizzle throws a grey-blue haze over everything. This is the time for planning. Get a modern book on the area you are going to visit, one with a good bibliography in the back, and order through your local library as many of the books listed as you can. Wade through them making notes of anything likely to be of photographic interest.

Straightforward pictures of well-known subjects such as the Cutty Sark are difficult to sell since they are produced in millions by the tourists. Here I tried to give some impression of how the riverside must have looked in Victorian times with sailing boats moored at the end of every street; it was just a question of walking around keeping the windjammer in view all the time until a worthwhile composition turned up. By all means take the obvious picture as soon as you see the subject, but then having got it off your chest start trying to get something off-beat and saleable.

Right up to 1868 public executions took place outside the nightmareish Newgate Prison (now the Old Bailey). On the night before the event the unfortunate condemned man was woken by the ringing of a handbell so that he could hear a pious poem being read—it must have been infuriating and went on from 1605 to 1840. Exploring the area I entered St. Sepulchre's, where people used to sleep overnight in the churchyard to get a front seat for the event, and was very suprised to come across the actual handbell in a glass case. Normally I would have photographed it by flash, holding it well to one side to avoid reflections from the glass, but to save bulk and weight I had stupidly left it at home. However, I did have the ever-useful monopod and was able to give a half second exposure in the dark church with reasonable success. Though I'm a great believer in research, you will come across all kinds of material purely by chance and must be prepared to take a picture even though conditions are difficult and you haven't brought the right apparatus.

Many of the illustrations will be hopelessly out of date, and much of the information will no longer apply. I once spent an afternoon in Kent looking for the ruins of a Norman keep which had been mentioned in three up-to-date guides, with a complete lack of success. Enquiring at the local pub, always the source of all knowledge in the country, I was told the last traces of it had disappeared in 1920; the writers had simply copied their information from older guide books without checking.

You will also find that many of the subjects illustrated in travel books can no longer be taken due to building and development. These days the changes happen very quickly and I have several times re-visited some glorious view or outstanding building that I had photographed perhaps five years before only to find it masked by a new factory, housing estate or motorway. However, all is grist to the working photographer's mill and I often take a picture from the previous position I had used, to illustrate the decline of rural Britain, the spoilation of the environment, etc., since "before" and "after" pictures make a very saleable pair. You have to learn how to turn disaster into advantage if you wish to survive.

If you can possibly manage a preliminary reconnaissance of the area it will be invaluable. Don't hesitate to tell the people you encounter what you are trying to do; many take a great interest and pride in their surroundings and will tell you where to find all kinds of useful subject matter. Best of all, if you can meet a local historian, perhaps a schoolmaster or the vicar, you can learn about the associations which make an otherwise dull object of great interest. Even if, at worst, you don't make any personal contacts you can at least check locations, camera positions, lighting, etc. so that when you come to actually take the pictures you can do so without delay. On the other hand the preliminary visit will take up useful time and almost double your overheads.

Maps

You must learn how to read maps and take time to study them before you set off. The Ordnance Survey ones are the most generally useful, the 1:50,000 ($1\frac{1}{4}''$ to the mile) "Landranger" series being the most generally useful if you are covering a large area by car, the 1:25,000 ($2\frac{1}{2}''$ to the mile) or the 1:10,000 "Pathfinder" ones being more suited to the walker and showing more detail.

The obvious use for maps is to take you to your destination along quiet and interesting country roads, often faster than the traffic-choked main routes. But in addition to this maps can show you where to find orchards in the spring and woods in autumn, tell you when the sunlight will fall on a village in a valley and the best time of day to photograph a stately home, guide you along footpaths to high ground overlooking a stretch of country, help you to locate streams and bridges to use as a foreground and generally give you a mental picture of the area you are going to explore.

Of course it isn't always an accurate one and this adds to the fun (and if you cease to get fun out of photography you should turn to some other profession). The village church you hoped would provide a centre of interest may turn out to be a Victorian monstrosity, the footpaths may be blocked with barbed wire and the bridge may be of the Bailey variety, but most of the time the map does give you a good idea of what you will encounter. I would never start off on an expedition without studying my maps very carefully.

Town plans are equally useful if you are photographing a built-up area, showing you

Pageants usually provide a wealth of subjects but if the people know they are being photographed they will automatically become self-conscious—you will need all the skill you possess in taking pictures unobserved. Automatic exposure setting is useful and autofocusing even more so, but don't worry if your camera has neither. The exposure will remain more or less constant with similar types of subject provided the light comes from behind the camera or to one side, and with practice manual focusing should not take more than $1\frac{1}{2}$ to 2 seconds. Alternatively focus on something the same distance away as the subject, swing round and press the release as soon as you have the picture on the screen.

Cibber's monument, made for the Sackville family in Withyham Church, East Sussex, is so astonishing and extraordinary that the temptation is to photograph the whole of it, showing the father and mother kneeling on cushions gazing at their dead 13 year old son. This should be taken for the record, but has been done so often in the past that it would hardly be saleable. To obtain impact it is much better to concentrate on just a part, in this case the son holding a skull and the upper half of the mother.

A 90 mm lens brought them closer together by compressing the perspective, and a tripod allowed a stop of f11 and an exposure of 1/8th of a second to be used with medium speed film—it was one of those occasions when carrying a tripod in the boot of the car paid off. The white marble gave such a long range of tones that a lot of holding back the shadows and printing in the highlights was needed when making the print. Had I been using colour I would have had to throw some light into the shadows by using a sheet of matte silver reflecting material I also carry folded in the boot, but the natural effect of the lighting might have been destroyed.

the short cuts and alleys which take you quickly to a location and are often interesting in themselves. For London I use the Geographers' *Master Atlas of Greater London*, a 3" to the mile book of maps covering all the suburbs as well as London itself. It is too big to carry easily but repays every minute of study on days when photography is impossible, saving a surprising amount of time and legwork.

Since a car in the average city is an embarrassing handicap, you are best to travel if possible on foot or if the distance is too great by bus or Underground. Maps for these are easily obtained and are invaluable for the stranger.

Checking The Equipment

No matter how familiar you are with your outfit, no matter how recently you have used it, it must become a matter of routine to check every item the evening before you set out. Test the batteries (they die without warning) and check also your spare. Cameras should be left on "Automatic" so that they can be brought into action without delay—if the last time you used them they were set on "Manual" you may miss a picture while you adjust the shutter. Lenses should be left set at an average stop, perhaps f5.6, film stock must be examined to make sure you have the right amount of the right emulsions. If you are going to use flash make sure the control is set on "X" and not "M" if it is adjustable—I doubt if there is a long-term professional in the land who hasn't as some time shot a roll using electronic flash with the control accidentally moved to the flashbulb setting, resulting in a series of blanks.

If you have bought a lens from an independent manufacturer, especially one with an interchangeable mount, check that when fitted to your camera it does not foul the head of the tripod or monopod. With some small cameras the mount may come down below the baseplate, which doesn't matter when the camera is handheld but which can cause a jam when on a support. Make sure the filters you have packed are of the correct size and check them for dust and fingerprints if they have been used recently.

If you own more than one make of camera make sure that the long focus and wide angle lenses fit the camera body you are carrying. Only a complete idiot would mix them up, as I said to myself when having driven two hundred miles to photograph an otter sanctuary in Norfolk I found I had a Minolta body and Olympus long focus lenses—luckily the charming little creatures were friendly enough for me to get close with a 50 mm. Don't think that experienced photographers never make mistakes; they make plenty but are cunning enough to overcome the effects.

Before you set out the question may arise "Should I take a companion?". If you just want to spend a day wandering around the countryside taking the odd picture if a suitable subject turns up, a companion may well add to your pleasure but if you are trying to do some serious photography it is better both for you and for your comrade if you are on your own. If like so many photographers you are completely absorbed in your work the companion will quickly become bored and irritated as you walk backwards and forwards, run up a hill to look at a view and then run down again without taking a picture, mutter to yourself, keep stopping to look through the viewfinder and generally behave selfishly.

If on the other hand you make polite conversation and generally try to be entertaining and considerate your mind will not be on the photography and your work will suffer greatly. A paid assistant is resigned to being treated as an accessory and doesn't resent being ignored but a friend expects different treatment. I feel that photography is a solitary pursuit demanding complete and utter concentration.

It is annoying to have to stop work to look for a restaurant or cafe so I usually carry some kind of packed meal—a flask of coffee, sandwiches, fruit and possibly chocolate though it tends to make you thirsty. A lunch break in a quiet pub can be very pleasant and relaxing but the inevitable drink will slow you down for the rest of the day; it's best to wait until you get home in the evening since landscape work calls for all the energy you possess.

Getting There

If you drive, the problem is to reach a country destination feeling as fresh and relaxed as possible and without wasting time on the road. For people living in large cities the only solution in summer is to leave home early enough to avoid the lemming-like torrent of commuters. In London for instance, if you leave around 6 a.m. you can drive through deserted streets and be starting photography by 7.30, 70 miles away, with little difficulty; wait until 7.30 before departing and the same journey can very easily take you at least $2\frac{1}{2}$ hours and you arrive tense and tired. Organise everything the evening before and get through town onto a motorway as early as possible, then branch onto country roads to reach the chosen area.

There is of course no such thing as the ideal car for the photographer any more than there is the ideal camera. A large, powerful vehicle is relaxing to drive and moves quickly on the main roads but can be difficult to handle in country lanes and hard to park in tight spaces. A small, agile one is fine in town or once you are in the country but tiring for long journeys. When you reach the location you will appreciate being able to raise the rear door of an estate car and sit on the back while you spread out your equipment, change films, pull on rubber boots, have a coffee and so on. But when you have to leave your car for any length of time you prefer a saloon with a boot in which you can lock equipment out of sight.

In winter the light will not be good enough for photography until the rush hour is almost over and after driving a long way in the dark and coping with the traffic you won't be in the mood to take good pictures. Under these conditions it is wiser to take a train or bus and limit the area you can cover to the distance you can walk. Since you will be travelling in the opposite direction to the rush you will be uncrowded, but these days it is essential to study an up to date timetable, especially when using country buses.

When you return home in the summer you can avoid the evening rush by starting off in the early afternoon, though this limits the amount of work you can do, or else in the evening at sunset, which lets you make use of the superb light cast by the low evening sun. Of course if you live in the country or can stay in a hotel for a while the whole problem of travelling is solved and you can take pictures from dawn to dusk.

Some people feel a bicycle can provide an answer, with town dwellers cycling to a station and letting the train take them and their bicycle to somewhere in the area they want to cover. The equipment is usually carried in the saddle bag to avoid vibration, with perhaps a tripod strapped to the crossbar; cycling with a gadget bag round your neck is inviting disaster. Once in the country this is a quiet and pleasant way of travelling, but it has its limitations since you will not want to leave your cycle unattended for very long

Apart from their importance as records, there is always a market for pictures of shops and crafts that have survived from the past. Shaplands in Holborn, for instance, have a shopfront and display that has little changed for a century or more; transparencies of this and similar old-established businesses can be sold many times abroad as well as in this country.

Using a 50mm lens it would have been necessary to step back into the road to include the whole of the shopfront, but if you tried this in Holborn your chances of survival would be minimal! There are two alternatives, either to stand on the opposite side of the street, use a long focus lens (a zoom would let you compose tightly without altering your position) and wait for a break in the traffic, or else switch to a wide angle one and stay on the pavement outside the shop. However it is essential to include suitable window-shoppers in a subject of this type since without them the picture would be dead and boring.

while you explore footpaths looking for fresh angles.

Walking undoubtedly gives you the greatest sense of freedom since you don't have to continually return to your car and don't have to worry about the safety of your cycle. With the intelligent use of timetables you can walk across country from one railway station or bus route to another without having to retrace your steps, but it really is essential to keep equipment to a minimum. If you are going any distance there is a lot to be said for carrying just a single compact SLR with equally compact long focus and wide angle lenses in the pockets of a field jacket, leaving the gadget bag at home.

The Lighting and the Seasons

Travelling around Britain it is hard to believe the light could vary so much in quality in such a small island. The cut glass clarity you sometimes get in the West Highlands that makes you think you can see to infinity; the pearly opalescence of a Suffolk sky; the autumn haze of burning leaves in a London square; the misty diffusion of an early morning in the Weald—I sometimes think that if I were taken in a closed van to any part of Britain I'd know where I was just from the lighting. No wonder this country can supply such an extraordinary variety of pictures.

There is no close season for photography in Britain. At any time of the year you can get spells of weather during which outdoor work is almost impossible due to a dank, blue-grey haze that flattens everything but on the other hand even in midwinter you get days of brilliant yellow sunshine when detail stands out very clearly. Every season of the year has its own unique advantages and you need never stop taking pictures for more than a few days at a time.

Spring brings the stormy, showery weather in which buildings and distant villages are often lit by a shaft of brilliant sunlight against a background of black storm clouds. The trees have only a light dusting of leaves, not enough to obscure long-distance views while in orchard country the pink and white blossom, not as easy to photograph as you might think, provides picture-postcard transparencies. Such subjects are very familiar and corny but they sell regularly; so it is up to you to make them more interesting and eye-catching than the next one. Make use also of the stretches of bluebells and daffodils which appear at this time of year, perhaps using a wide angle lens and taking a close-up of a clump with the rest forming a background, or else using a long focus one to compress perspective and bring a widely spaced carpet of flowers together into a compact mass. Early spring also has the considerable advantage that the holiday-makers have not yet arrived and the country and its roads are comparatively empty.

In most parts of Britain summer brings lush foliage and in a wooded area you have to climb high to photograph a stretch of country, otherwise you won't see beyond the next tree. If I wanted to take a long distance view over the Weald, for instance, I would do so either from the South Downs in Sussex or the North Downs in Kent; once you are on lower ground the leaves limit the picture. In theory the long hours of sunlight should make photography possible from perhaps 6 a.m to 10 p.m. but most people taking landscapes stop in the middle of the morning, starting again in the late afternoon.

A showery day in Kent with the sky changing from light to dark within seconds—it seemed a good opportunity to take a useful stock shot of Aylesford. However, the Medway which runs through the village is a tidal river and not having done my homework I arrived there when the water was low, exposing the muddy banks and an assortment of rubbish. For more than a century pictures of Aylesford were taken from the bank to the East of the bridge, but as so-called development has made this position difficult to reach I moved along to the other side, including the church, the 14th century bridge and the row of riverside houses. The only problem was to avoid the mud so I fitted the invaluable 24mm lens and crouched low, using the weeds and flowers on the bank both as a screen and to give depth to the picture.

The wider the angle of the lens the more apparent movement is given to the clouds in the sky, but care has to be taken to keep the back of the camera vertical since even the slightest tilt will give a "falling over backwards" effect to the buildings. It is always worth looking at a scene through the viewfinder with the camera held as high and as low as possible before taking the picture. It may well be that the normal eye level position gives the best result, but try other angles first.

Every year the senior members of the Bar attend a service at Westminster Abbey and then march in procession to a reception in the House of Lords, a colourful and rather frightening sight. The procession is photographed by a handful of bored pressmen and a million or so amateur photographers; the problem was to find a new approach to the event.

Legal friends told me when the judges would start to arrive in Dean's Yard at the side of the Abbey, so I got there well ahead of time and fitted a 100 mm lens to the Minolta XE-1, 1972 vintage but utterly reliable, which I use for a lot of my work. It was loaded with Kodachrome 64 and the light was poor, so I appreciated the good definition given by the lens at the large apertures necessary at the 1/250th I use as a minimum speed for candid work with this focal length. Apart from the judges I was the only person present so I concealed myself behind a tree and took a series of shots of the arrivals in off-guard moments.

A row of tug-boat propellors and a couple of oil storage tanks may not seem very promising material and had the picture been taken at midday the result would have been boring. However if you wander round industrial sites and docks just before sunset the low lighting can transform the most ordinary scene. You have at most half an hour in which to get your pictures, and you have to be generous with your exposure since the light is less actinic than it appears to the eye. Selenium and CdS meters tend to be over-sensitive to the red end of the spectrum and may react too strongly to the orange light from the setting sun; it is wise to make a second exposure giving a stop more than the meter suggests.

Meanwhile they concentrate on interiors, the reason being of course that the high sun kills detail and modelling by being too directly overhead.

A warm day in summer is often followed by a misty morning and as the haze starts to clear the soft, diffused sunlight becomes ideal for colour work, the differences in the colours of the subject providing the necessary contrast. The lighting may well be too soft for black and white work for which I prefer the long, sharp-edged shadows and the greater clarity of the evening.

For the colour worker autumn is probably the most active time of the year, when the rather monotonous green of the trees changes to a variety of golds and browns. Stubble burns in the harvested fields, the woods are carpeted with fallen leaves, the roads are once more empty and the light forms shadows and shapes throughout the day. With the crops safely in, the people you meet are more relaxed and have time to talk, you can carry equipment for long distances without getting too hot, and the tourists have gone. Because the days are shorter, this would be a good time of the year to stay at a hotel in the area you are going to cover to avoid the rush-hour travelling which would otherwise be inevitable.

The sun shines more often than you would think in winter, and though landscapes can appear bleak unless you include some bold foreground object it is a good time to photograph buildings since the low sunlight exaggerates texture and detail. When snow falls the most ordinary scenes are transformed but are only worth photographing on sunny days, otherwise the snow appears as a stretch of dull grey. There is always a market for pictures of crisp, sparkling winter scenes but if possible a human should be included to give life and a centre of interest.

Blowy, gusty conditions often make landscape work difficult since the leaves and branches swing about and are often hard to record sharply unless they are a long way off. A useful alternative technique is to mount the camera on a steady tripod, load with slow film if possible, stop the lens right down and give an exposure of a second or two—if using black and white material the addition of an orange or red filter will increase the exposure needed considerably. The leaves will now appear as a blur, conveying the impression of a windy day and often adding interest to an otherwise dull scene.

The difficulty in this country with its changeable weather is to plan your expedition well in advance—it's of little use to know what conditions will be like today if you intend taking pictures in three days time. I find the long range weather forecast that follows the "Farmers Programme" on Sundays on the TV gives a surprisingly accurate account of the weather over the whole of the country for the coming week—it should be required viewing for all outdoor photographers.

Incidentally, throughout this book I have stressed taking pictures that will sell but there is much more to photography than this. You must try to introduce some self-expression, some individual way of looking at conventional objects—if you take pictures that bore you simply because you think they will sell you can be quite sure the picture editor will find them boring as well. Subjects taken in sunlight may be more in demand than ones taken in bad weather but if you see something that interests you, photograph it whatever the conditions—if it genuinely interests you it will probably interest other people as well.

From the practical point of view, when we are planning to photograph an area we should study the map and first of all list the eastward-facing places—houses, castles, villages, landscapes—that will best be photographed in the morning, tackling these before,

If Bodiam hadn't existed Kodak would have built it! More film is exposed on this fairy-tale castle than on any other subject in the British countryside. It is probably true to say that it has been photographed at least a million times, and to produce something new and saleable was no easy undertaking. The weather was ideal for colour work with white clouds reflecting light into the shadows to lower the contrast. At the time the moat was full of water lilies and it looked as though they could provide a bold foreground if I could get close enough to a few of them, using a super-wide lens to give a startling perspective.

In order to make the water lilies appear large I had to position the camera only a few inches away, wading into the moat, which has banks that are both steep and slippery, whilst a group of village children gathered to watch with interest the novelty of a suicide attempt taking place!

It's always wise to keep a loaded camera near at hand just in case a subject appears unexpectedly—it doesn't happen very often but when it does you want to go into action without delay. Glancing out of my sitting room window one morning I saw to my surprise a balloon floating serenely over Hampstead Heath—it made a pleasant change to have a picture come to me instead of having to search for it.

I had been testing a 50–250mm f4/f5.6 Tokina zoom which was still fitted to a camera loaded with Kodachrome 64. Setting it to the longest focal length the maximum aperture of f5.6 made a shutter speed of 1/125th necessary in the weak early morning light. This is too slow a speed for satisfactory handheld work at 250mm but by resting the lens on the window ledge a sharp result was obtained.

There is of course nothing very interesting or saleable about a picture of a hot air balloon, but when one floats over Hampstead Heath the picture can be sold to a number of North London local papers (most of them use colour these days) and possibly to a National.

On the whole I prefer "straight" lenses to zooms, adjusting the distance between the camera and the subject to compose the picture, but this was a perfect example of the advantage of being able to adjust the focal length.

Though I prefer unposed portraits some subjects can provide an equally effective result even though they are quite aware they are being photographed. It helps considerably to strike up a conversation so that they realise you are friendly and harmless and then to ask them politely if they'd mind if you took a picture. Most people like to have their place of work included—in the case of a butcher it might be his shop, a fisherman would wish to have his boat in the background, a vicar his church or in this case the flower seller was quite proud of her stall. The lighting here is harsh, direct sunlight but this helps to convey the character of the subject.

If working in black and white always make a gift of a few prints whether they are requested or not. It works wonders for future relations with the subject who will always co-operate if you need more pictures—in fact if you are shooting colour it pays to take a few black and whites as well just to give away. This is one of the reasons why you should carry two camera bodies if possible, loaded with the two types of material.

say, 11 a.m. Westward-facing subjects are taken in the late afternoon and evening, while in the middle of the day we concentrate on subjects in the shade and interiors. This is why accurate map-reading is so invaluable.

There are two kinds of weather which most outdoor photographers dread: the dull grey days which give no modelling at all and at the other end of the scale those with a clear, blue, cloudless sky when shadows become harsh and empty of detail, just as though the subject had been lit by a spotlight. The ideal day has a sky with plenty of white, puffy clouds that act just like large floating reflectors, throwing the sunlight into the shadows. Under these conditions you can occasionally take backlit landscapes and buildings that show shadow detail, but normally this type of lighting is avoided since backlit landscapes are very difficult to reproduce successfully in print.

For dramatic, eyecatching results, however, there is nothing to beat the stormy, showery weather of spring when so many photographers stay at home for fear of getting wet. The most ordinary subjects appear strange under the odd lighting with its sudden rays of sunshine and black clouds.

When the sun shines brilliantly from a clear blue sky, the snapshotters reach for their cameras while the experienced workers put theirs away. Working down in Cornwall, I had experienced a series of such days which had made photography very difficult. Then the storm clouds started to roll up and work could be resumed.

The classic landscape has a dark foreground, medium-toned middle distance and light background, but a reversal of these tones can make your picture more eye-catching. Here the lobster pots form a dark base to the subject, but the sun lights the ships in the middle distance brilliantly while the threatening sky background is dark. This could be useful for a magazine cover, since there is plenty of room for light-toned lettering at both top and bottom.

When taking long distance views of built-up areas and traffic-choked cities you will find that during the week the fumes from lorries, cars and industry throws a blue-grey haze over the scene if the air is at all still. For this reason it is best to work on Sunday evenings, ideally after rain followed by a stiff breeze has washed the air clean. Low sunlight will emphasise the detail.

Don't leave things to chance, make a list of locations from which you can get an uninterrupted long distance view so that when a suitable evening arrives you can go there without delay. Try if possible to follow the rules of colour composition—something red or orange in the foreground to provide a centre of interest followed by a green or yellow middle distance. Any lens can be used since they all have advantages and disadvantages; a wide angle one including lots of sky to give a feeling of space but making the buildings appear small and distant, while with a long focus one you can select an interesting section of the scene but increase the haze problem.

There is an element of luck in finding some warm-coloured object in the foreground (though I've known some smart-alec photographers use an assistant dressed in a red jacket) but this adds to the fun!

It is quite possible to include the sun in a picture provided it is low in the sky, since the haze that hangs just above the horizon will soften and diffuse the rays. The technique is most effective when a stretch of water gives a reflection and there are some back-lit clouds in the sky, but your lens must be as flare-free as possible. Some multi-element zooms for instance, though satisfactory in normal lighting, can produce a line of reflections, one from each element, right across the picture. If you expose according to the metering system the sky area and the water will probably be reproduced correctly with objects in silhouette, but it is wise to bracket so as to obtain a variety of effects.

Composition

A print or transparency is a two-dimensional representation of a three-dimensional subject. To make it appear as realistic as possible the conventional and very effective method when working in black and white is to have a dark foreground, a medium tone in the middle distance and a light background. With colour much the same applies, with the addition that there should preferably be a reddish object in the foreground (a red-painted tractor for example), the middle distance should be yellow or green (perhaps a cornfield) while the background is blue (distant hills). There is of course no hard and fast rule about this but if you can arrange the picture in this way it will have a feeling of depth.

This is why the black cloud backgrounds and bright, sunlit foregrounds of a stormy spring give us such a visual shock; it is the reverse of what we have come to expect.

Perspective also plays a big part in creating an illusion of depth, wide angle lenses tending to exaggerate the feeling (because we get very close to the subject) and long focus ones to reduce it (because we stand further away). However, the effect must be used with common sense. Suppose we are down in the docks photographing a cargo boat moored by a cable to a bollard. If we get close to the latter and use, say, a 24 mm lens on a 35 mm SLR the bollard will appear large and important with the cable apparently stretching a long way towards a small and insignificant ship. There will be a good feeling of depth but the picture will lack interest. Get well back, use a 135 mm lens and the bollard will appear small in comparison to the vessel, as it is, and the boat will fill the frame, giving much more impact even though the perspective has been flattened.

People talk in camera clubs about the "rules of composition" but there are of course no rules in photography, only ways of doing things that over the years have been found to produce satisfactory results. The classic, conventional way of arranging the elements of a picture has for many centuries been to divide the canvas or viewfinder into six equal rectangles by two imaginary upright lines and two horizontal ones. The points where these lines cross are known as the "strong points" of the picture and it is recommended that the main centre of interest should be positioned on one or the other. The horizon should run along either the upper or lower horizontal line, never across the centre, while a strong upright line such as a tree trunk should be positioned on one of the vertical ones. Roads, footpaths, streams, etc. should lead into the picture, not out of it, and landscapes are best framed by the branches of a tree or taken through an open gate. This has been the conventional advice given to landscape workers ever since photography began and it still works very well provided you—and the picture editors—like conventional landscapes.

Novices would be wise to work in this way until they have gained experience and confidence. Then if faced with a vast, dramatic sky in the flat Romney Marsh they may decide to position the horizon below the imaginary bottom horizontal line; if they are taking a wide angle picture along the furrows of a ploughed field they might place the horizon above the upper line. Photographing a ship head on, the vertical line of the bow could well run up the exact centre of the picture to give extra impact and you could do the same with a railway track. By all means stick to conventional composition for most of your pictures but don't be afraid to break the "rules" if you feel the result will be more interesting.

After a while, of course, you will no longer think about "dividing thirds" or "strong points" but will compose the picture in the most effective way quickly and instinctively. I know it's a cliché but there really is no substitute for experience.

Colour transparencies must be composed as tightly as possible with as little unwanted space around the edges as possible (zoom lenses can help you do this). You have a little more latitude with black and white negatives but for maximum quality the composition must still be as tight as possible. You must get your eye close enough to the viewing lens of the finder to be able to see all four edges of the frame at the same time. Some people, especially spectacle wearers, never do this and consequently never make use of the full available area of the film. The difficulty can often be overcome by the use of "eyepiece correction lenses" that fit onto the rear of the finder to make spectacles unnecessary.

A constant composition problem with all cameras except the stand variety is that of "converging verticals". When photographing a tall building the temptation is to tilt the camera backwards to include the top, with the result that the building appears to be falling over backwards. No one will buy such a picture unless the effect is exaggerated and dramatic, so it is important to know how to overcome this problem.

The further away you get the less tilt is needed and if there is sufficient space for you to use a 135 mm lens on a 35 mm camera and still include the whole of the building, the amount by which the verticals converge will hardly be noticeable. However, to have such a space is unusual; as often as not you have to stay close. The answer then is to fit a wide angle lens, keep the camera back as upright as possible and position the building in the upper part of the viewfinder. If you are using black and white and have a lens of top quality closed down to a medium stop you should be able to make a satisfactory print from the upper part of the negative. However, this will not work with colour, where it is far better to use the same technique but find something appropriate with which to fill the otherwise empty foreground. A flowery garden would be suitable for a cottage, a moat filled with water lilies for a castle, some farm implements or an old cart for a barn—all very conventional but saleable. Use whatever is available but avoid blank stretches of grass or paving.

For some 35 mm SLR cameras "perspective control" lenses are available which can be moved up and down and sideways to give exactly the same effect as the rising and shifting front on a stand camera. These let you hold the camera back vertically, without tilt, and still include the top of a building. They can produce prints and transparencies of outstanding quality since the whole of the available film area is used. However, they are very expensive (the lens has to have extraordinary covering power and the mount is complicated and precision made) and need time if they are going to be used to best advantage. Most

Built around 1750, Halnaker Mill is simple, unpretentious and very pleasant in the early morning sunlight of a spring day. The view from the hilltop stretches for miles along the coast and since the climb to reach it is steep you usually have the place to yourself. However I feel that buildings such as this need a figure in the foreground to bring life and depth to the subject, so I lugged a tripod with me to the summit. Setting up the camera with a wide angle lens I included an old stile and then, setting the self timer, galloped forwards to include myself in the picture. Unfortunately the mud was incredibly slippery and I slid about hearing the shutter click before I could reach the stile. After several attempts I finally got there in time, but it was a close run thing!

The background and surroundings of a portrait are often just as important and convey just as much information as the subject. This quarryman was photographed with a 35mm lens in order to include the conveyer belts and the building housing the stone crusher; normally I would use a semi-long focus lens for portraiture. According to the "rules of composition" the head should have been on a dividing third but positioning it centrally helped to convey the strength and solidity of the subject.

photographers will have to use the "wide angle lens and fill the foreground" technique, but a perspective control lens might well be justified if you are going to specialise in 35 mm transparencies of architecture.

So far we have stressed the importance of tight composition when using colour, especially in the case of 35 mm, but this really applies to pictures that are going to be reproduced in books, magazines, calendars, etc. If you are hoping to sell your work for use on magazine covers or for use in advertising (both paying well), you have to remember that titles and lettering will be superimposed on your picture and that it must not block out any vital part of the subject. Having taken your tightly composed picture it is therefore wise to recompose it so that an area is left at the top to take lettering, perhaps the sky, with a darker part, possibly a heavy shadow or a ploughed field at the base to take information in white (reversed) lettering. You can then offer the purchaser a choice of usage, important if you are selling your material through a picture agency. It is much easier to do this if you are using medium format since the bigger area gives you more latitude in composition.

People in Pictures

Nothing adds to the interest of a picture so much as the inclusion of a human being. People like to look at pictures of other people and the first thing that catches their eye, the main focus of their attention, is always a person in a landscape, no matter how distant. Ideally the figure should be appropriate to its surroundings and if, for instance, you are photographing a country church it is worth going to some trouble to include the vicar, someone scything the grass, a sale of work—anything to give human interest. Don't ignore the obvious—a fisherman painting his boat sounds as corny as a farmer shearing sheep but they can both sell.

Try to avoid tourists, who will usually appear out of place. On occasion I have placed the camera on a tripod, set the self-timer and galloped on to a dividing third, hoping that a rear view of someone wearing a field jacket would be fairly neutral. Needless to say, in order to be seen the figure must differ in colour and tone from the background—someone in a brown corduroy jacket would merge into autumn leaves while a clergyman wearing a light grey suit would be invisible against the stone walls of a church. It seems obvious, but when working under pressure, as you will be if you turn professional, it is easy to forget to place light against dark and warm colours against cold ones.

If using a wide angle lens don't position the figure near the edge of the frame when holding the camera horizontally since this will result in apparent distortion. This is especially true with super wides, when the figure should be near the central area.

People As The Main Subject

As you travel around Britain you will come across people engaged in odd and photographable occupations, some very unlikely indeed. It is, of course, no use hoping to stumble on them by chance; you find them by general reading and by asking local people. Britain is changing so rapidly that the information will often be out of date—I was a month too late to photograph the last flint-knapper in Norfolk, the Sussex baker who heated his oven with faggots of wood had just gone over to gas, the man in Kent who cured snake skins had retired—but if you persevere you will gather a lot of useful material. Provided

While writing and illustrating an article about a firm of bow-makers who work in Sherwood Forest, the usual pictures were taken of the various stages in manufacture and some of the surrounding countryside. However human interest was essential to bring life to the story. Using a 100 mm lens at f4 to throw the background out of focus, I took some close-up portraits in harsh sunlight of someone using one of the products. Picture stories of manufacturing are often visually boring and it is essential to include pictures of people, the more bold and obvious the better.

Street market photography is a fairly easy business—there are lots of characters, too busy to take much interest in the man with the camera, and since the stalls are in straight lines once you have focused on one the focus will probably be correct for the rest, as will the exposure. All you have to do is to walk down the line raising the camera whenever you see a good subject. If there is enough space a medium long focus lens lets you stand well back—here a 90 mm Tamron was used.

you can accompany your pictures with extended captions or short articles you can sell them to a wide range of journals, not just trade or local ones.

A typical example would be that of Mr Gandolfi. Long before he became well-known I heard rumours that he was still making traditional mahogany and brass cameras of superb quality in South London. My first letters brought no reply but I continued asking to meet him. Eventually he agreed to let me photograph him at work, we became friends, he made me the finest 5″ × 4″ stand camera in the world, and when the pictures were published TV crews, photographers and journalists started to arrive until producing programmes and articles about him became almost an industry in itself—all because I kept on writing to him.

You can't gather too much miscellaneous information. Local papers, reference books and just ordinary gossip will supply a lot of clues to be followed—it was through conversation that I photographed a firm of bow-makers in Sherwood Forest and the last lamp-lighter in London, who appears at dusk in the Temple. Farriers, wheelwrights, coopers, collectors of vintage aircraft or cars or bicycles, bell-ringers, picture restorers—subject matter is never far away. However, in most cases there must be some handle on which to hang the pictures and the story. In the case of bell-ringers, for instance, it might be that the team included the youngest or the oldest enthusiast in the country or else some well-known personality. Alternatively an ancient bell might have been re-cast or a sponsored ringing record might be attempted. The belfry might have been recently restored or still be lit by oil lamps—you must try to find some interesting angle since a straightforward picture of bell-ringers has no news value.

This kind of work calls for all your lighting and portrait experience. Outdoor portraiture in daylight is comparatively simple, but indoors if the natural light is unsuitable it is best to use at least two and preferably three flash units, triggered by photocells. Try to arrange matters so that the subject is facing the main source of light, which should come from one side to give shape and modelling.

In order to avoid self-consciousness on the part of the subject it is best to photograph him while he is working at his craft. He is probably proud of his skill and will be glad to demonstrate and talk about it and this is the time to take the pictures. On no account say "Hold it!" or do anything to make him pause—there is no danger of subject movement with flash and if, for instance, he stops in the middle of planing a piece of wood while the shutter is released the result will inevitably look posed and static even though in theory it should not.

As with all portrait work you must establish a rapport with the subject as quickly as possible. Always tell them what you are doing and ask them politely if they would mind having their picture taken. Don't be too serious about it and at all costs be completely familiar with your apparatus so that you don't have to think about it; 90% of your attention must be on the subject. Even if you are working in colour take a few black and whites as well so that you can send him some prints—I know it's a bit of a chore, especially when you are busy, but send them off as soon as possible (make sure you take the correct name and address at the time). This pays off remarkably well and has brought me many friends amongst the craftsmen of Britain who are always ready to be photographed again and who have passed on much useful information. Never, ever, say you'll send pictures and then fail to do so—it queers the pitch for all photographers in the future.

In addition to arranged pictures you will of course want to take unposed ones—candids if you like—at agricultural shows, fairs and local ceremonies where you will encounter some extraordinary characters. The ideal camera for this work is probably the auto-focusing SLR since you simply raise it to your eye, compose as quickly as possible and press the release but if you don't possess one don't worry—you can take good unposed pictures with any camera.

A technique that has been almost forgotten is to learn how to estimate just a couple of distances accurately, perhaps five and fifteen feet. You won't need more than these for your purpose and it takes years of practice to guess all distances. Set the focusing scale on your lens to one or the other and then simply move backwards and forwards until the camera is in the right position. However, most people like to depend on their rangefinder or microprism, but if you focus on the subject by this means there will be a slight delay before you take the picture, of perhaps one or one and a half seconds in the case of an experienced operator.

A quicker and possibly more accurate technique is to first of all focus on a fixed object such as a gate post and then wait until the subject comes level with it. Alternatively, focus on something the same distance away as the subject but at right angles to it and then swing round quickly, compose and press.

Back in the days when the twin-lens Rollei was the standard professional camera we used to carry it hanging by its strap from one shoulder down by our side, one hand holding it casually with a finger on the release. A glance down at the screen from time to time let us check that the subject was centred and then the shutter would be released while we were looking directly at the subject's pose and expression rather than at the camera—they never realised they had been photographed.

Try to become as invisible as possible. Move slowly, dress conventionally and stand if possible in shadow with the sun behind you. Shutter speeds must be high enough to stop movement on the part of the subject, but on the other hand a smallish stop will be needed to give enough depth of field to cover small focusing errors. These two things are contradictory unless you use a 400 ASA film, but if you prefer the better quality given by slower emulsions and are not using an auto-focusing camera you can still use a medium or large aperture successfully if you first of all choose a good setting for your picture. Choose an archway, a flight of steps, the entrance to a marquee or a barn and then pre-focus carefully on the spot where you want to position your subject. When he gets there press the release and the result must be dead sharp. You may have to wait for some time for the right person to come along but you'll be sure of the result.

Curiosities

Nothing sells so steadily as pictures of the odd and unusual objects and events you will come across in your travels. Every editor likes to hold a stock of such subjects ready to fill the unexpected empty space that crops up when an advertisement is cancelled or an article fails to turn up on time, and pictures I took thirty years ago are still being used.

The only real problem is to find the subjects, and as usual a lot of research both at home and in the field will be necessary. History books and old guides are useful, but nothing beats local knowledge since the most ordinary-looking objects often have an extraordinary story or association behind them. Visit every small museum you come across and talk to the curator, usually a mine of useful information. Always examine the little

Conventional pictures of places like Brixham Harbour just don't sell, since so many thousands of them are produced every year by the tourists. It is better to concentrate on a small area of activity—in this case a fisherman cleaning his boat—a 90mm lens being used to obtain a tight composition. Backlighting helped the spray of water to stand out and a shutter speed of 1/250th at f5.6 was fast enough to stop most of the movement. The red paint on the hull helps to sell the picture; people always like warm colours in outdoor summer scenes and had the hull been green or blue the result would have had little impact.

Well within living memory the lamp-lighters setting off on their bicycles at dusk to light the gas-powered lampposts was one of the sights of London. Electricity has made them obsolete but little pockets of gas lamps survive. Such a one exists in the Temple, the legal area, and a porter told me when and where the lamp-lighter, one of the very few left, would start work. Using a 35 mm lens, just enough exposure was given to record the lamp; correct exposure for the rest of the subject would have destroyed the effect. I of course got into conversation with the lamp-lighter beforehand and asked his permission—politeness always pays off.

locally-printed posters on trees and telegraph poles beside the road announcing fairs, auctions, gymkhanas, church sales of work, etc. and make a note of the dates and locations (don't rely on your memory since by the time you have returned home you will have forgotten the details).

Explore also churches and churchyards, which often provide a lot of interesting material, and buy the church guide which costs little but often tells you a lot. Incidentally, some photographers have the idea that because a church is a meeting place for the public they are at liberty to take what pictures they please, but it is really private property and the vicar is quite at liberty to ban photography if he wishes, usually as the result of bad behaviour on the part of a photographer or photographers in the past. If on entering a church you see a clergyman, a verger or anyone vaguely official, always ask very politely if you may take pictures, explaining your interest. I have only been refused once and even then after a few minutes conversation I was told I could take what I liked. Try to understand their point of view.

The general rule is that you can photograph anything you can see from the road, footpath or other public ground. However, possession of a camera does not give you permission to trespass. If the only way to photograph a building is from the private grounds or garden, knock at the door and ask. Most owners are flattered and helpful.

Though research is so essential, many curious objects and happenings will be encountered by sheer chance. The incredible Waggoners War Memorial at Sledmere in Yorkshire, the unique gravestones at Ayr in Scotland, the procession of cricketers carrying a spit-roasted sheep at Ebernoe Horn Fair in Sussex, the pub at Balls Cross that becomes a polling-booth at elections, the graveyard at Gracehill in Northern Ireland in which men are buried on one side and women on the other, and the wall painting of the red-haired St Uncumber upside-down in Burton church all came as a surprise, as did much similar material.

Never be afraid to re-photograph a subject that has already been used to illustrate a guide book, since with modern equipment and a fresh, individual way of looking at things you may produce something new and exciting. Remember that efficient super-wide lenses, for instance, didn't exist until some twenty years ago and there are many subjects that cannot be properly tackled without them. The thousand skulls in the crypt in Hythe make a good example; they must have been photographed many times for many years but without a 17 mm lens on a 35 mm camera it is impossible to show the full gruesome Gothic horror of the effect.

The fishing boats of Hastings have been photographed over and over again—they make an irresistible subject. Unless you produce a result with exceptional impact such pictures are difficult to sell by themselves since the subject is so familiar, but when accompanied by an interesting and informative article it's another matter.

In this case for instance, you could write about the unique Fisherman's Quarter with its tall, tarred net sheds; about the harbour that was swept away by storms so that the boats have to be hauled up onto the beach; the French Connection through inter-marriage; the way in which the fish are sold by Dutch auction; the kinds of fish that are caught at different periods of the year; the past and possibly present smuggling; the fishermen's pubs; the extinct boat-building industry—with only a little research you could accompany a selection of pictures with a very readable article and have it published with several illustrations instead of selling just a single transparency.

Willy Lott's cottage has become a joke amongst generations of landscape photographers since for very many years no photographic exhibition was complete without at least one example. Near Flatford Mill in Suffolk, it is peered at and photographed by hundreds of thousands of people every year and because of this it has been ignored by many professional photographers of the countryside. There is however a constant demand for good pictures of this type of subject, however corny, and it is a mistake to ignore the obvious. The pictures taken by the tourists never reach the market and anyway can rarely compete with those taken by an experienced worker. A dead calm day and still water let me include a perfect reflection of the building; the dark foreground and the clear sky area allows lettering to be added if necessary.

Every city can provide almost unknown ceremonies that have rarely been photographed—finding out when and where they take place is fun and can help you build up useful contacts. The annual procession of the Vintners Society is a good example, probably stretching back to the Middle Ages. In front a porter sweeps the street with a besom (probably essential up to the turn of the century), officials and dignitaries carry nosegays of flowers to kill the smell of the mob, and the whole thing is very odd and very British. This is the kind of moving subject for which an auto-focusing camera is a great advantage, otherwise you have to pre-focus on a mark on the ground and wait for the subject to reach it. I obtained details of the procession by phoning the Vintners Society—direct methods are usually best—and arriving early talked to the police to discover the exact route.

Townscape

There are just as many pictures to be taken in towns as in the country, in fact probably more. You don't have to go to a tourist centre—photos of the Concrete Cows of Milton Keynes are more saleable than ones of the Dreaming Spires of Oxford—because wherever you get a lot of people living in the same place you will find eccentrics and characters, odd customs and ceremonies.

In the big, old cities such as London the supply of material is inexhaustible and you can soon build up a library of worthwhile pictures without having to go very far. There is in fact a great deal to be said for specialising in a comparatively small area, so that if someone wants, for instance, examples of City Ceremonies he will automatically approach you since you are known to have a good selection. Just as anyone wanting transparencies of birds would get in touch with Eric Hosking, or with Don McCullin for war pictures so, once you are established, they will turn to you for your speciality.

As with country photography, it's not much use slinging your gadget bag over your shoulder and going for a long walk in the hope that something will turn up. The apparently casual shots of happenings are usually the result of careful planning, reading and general research.

To take an absolutely basic example, let's suppose you want a tourist-type picture of the Horse Guards riding along the Mall; professionals tend to ignore such obvious subjects and as a result really good examples sell readily. The first step is to find a location with a suitable background, perhaps the Duke of York's Steps with the column rising above them. Next decide on the focal length of lens that will include the right area of the scene. Since you will want the troop on your side of the road they will have to be returning to the Palace rather than coming away from it, so you next have to find out the time of day when this happens (it hardly varies). They move faster than you might think, so a shutter speed of about 1/500th will be needed with the stop set accordingly. Finally, having completed all this pre-planning you choose a day when the weather is kind, go to your selected position, focus on the spot in the road where you want the leader and then take the picture when he gets there. The result will look like the kind of snapshot every tourist imagines he can take but doesn't.

Detective work is required to a much greater extent if you want to record the odd and almost unknown ceremonies that take place in most old towns, especially in the City of London. The Livery Companies for example like to keep theirs almost private, and I have

The standard picture of St. Paul's is taken from the top of Ludgate Hill, showing the West front. The trouble is that if you work from street level you will inevitably have a foreground of tourist buses, traffic and visitors. If you can talk your way into one of the office blocks facing the Cathedral you can obtain a better view from a few floors up, but many of the windows are sealed and you cannot get good results, of course, taking the picture through glass.

I prefer to wander round the precincts trying to find a better foreground than a bus. In spring and summer there are plenty of flowers in bloom in beds to the South of the building, and by using a 17 mm Tamron and holding the camera a foot away from the flowers they make a colourful base to the picture.

Straightforward pictures of floodlit buildings can be very boring if they simply include the building and nothing else; a dark foreground leading into the subject is usually needed. A steady tripod is essential since exposures will be too long for the camera to be handheld, and consequently there is no need for fast film. An 18mm lens was used to exaggerate the perspective of the alley leading up to St. Paul's, the absence of people being due to the fact that the City is deserted late at night. Exposure was based on the floodlit Cathedral but increased sufficiently to give some shadow detail.

Most pictures of graffiti are not in demand because the subject is so familiar and hackneyed, but occasionally you come across something that will sell steadily over the years because it has a universal appeal. You don't need advanced equipment for this kind of work; a compact pocket camera is quite good enough provided the lens is of a reasonably high standard. If I am just walking for pleasure instead of being on a specific assignment I use an auto-compact as a note-taker in the same way that an artist carries a pencil and sketching pad. The camera need not necessarily have auto-focusing or even automatic exposure but such things are convenient and save time.

in fact sometimes been the only photographer present at their processions. The problem is, of course, to discover when and where they are held, and I have found that as usual the most direct and simple method is best—I simply telephone the Company concerned and ask them politely and humbly for details. The Tourist Board will also be able to help you, but much of your information will come from reading and from conversations with anyone likely to know about such matters.

Apart from the Livery Companies there are ceremonies connected with the Bar, the Corporation, the Church, schools, apprenticeships, the Thames, Parliament, hospitals and almshouses, the Forces—the enquiring photographer can discover a vast number if he is willing to do some hard research. Don't worry if some of them are familiar; it's up to you to photograph them in a new and interesting way.

I find it very useful to arrive at a location well before the event takes place, partly to find a good camera position but mainly to talk to the officials who are in charge of the arrangements, and the police. Make yourself agreeable and you can obtain a great deal of information about the route, the timing, any important people who are arriving and so on. Once you have struck up an acquaintance people can be surprisingly helpful but you must of course never become a nuisance and never get in the way. As always, the most successful photographers make themselves invisible.

There is also a rich mine of saleable pictures amongst the odd trades and crafts to be found in all big towns. Most people have photographed one or two but there are very few up to date comprehensive collections, the kind of thing a buyer of such material wants to see. This branch of town photography in particular calls for a lot of legwork, much wading through trade directories, many enquiries and a great deal of disappointment but it can pay off handsomely, always provided your results are of good quality.

Street markets and street photography generally will call for quick reactions and all your documentary skill. One of the main problems lies in accurate focusing and for this type of work auto-focusing cameras are of course ideal. However, you can obtain equally sharp and even faster results by pre-focusing. Suppose you are walking past a line of stalls and see an interesting character. Display no interest, carry on walking but mentally assess the position you will be in when you take the picture. Then, standing at the same distance from another stall, focus the lens on it and stroll back. As you come level with the subject whip up the camera and press the release. Alternatively, take up a position opposite the stall you want to photograph, focus, and then wait until the owner is busy with a customer.

If you are using a 35 mm camera, ideal for this kind of work, a standard 50 mm lens and a medium long focus one, something between 85 and 105 mm will be most useful. If you are using a zoom pre-set it to a suitable focal length—if you try to adjust it while actually taking the picture the delay will be too great.

Architectural photography is usually a good deal more difficult than in the country, though of course you have much more material. The problems are those of parked cars, the difficulty of getting a reasonable distance away from the subject, and the shadows cast on it by other buildings. As always, planning is necessary.

A large-scale map of the town will tell you which buildings are best taken in the mornings and which in the evening, depending of course on the direction in which they are facing. If you can manage to explore your town at dawn in summer you will find it transformed. Many streets will be almost empty of cars, the warm, low light will accentuate the detail on the buildings and there will be no people around to get in the way. It really is an

No one is going to buy a straightforward picture of a doss house, but when accompanied by the information that Stalin and Litvinov stayed there during a visit to London in 1908 it immediately becomes saleable. General reading and research always pays off—every photographer should have a mind that is a "ragbag of completely useless information" as mine was once described. When working in the tougher areas I carry my camera under my jacket and leave my gadget bag at home—it attracts unwanted attention. Having set the exposure and focus I put the camera away until a suitable person came along, whipping up the camera and pressing the release as he walked into the picture.

Most towns have their buskers and most are very willing to be photographed—provided you start off by letting them see you make a decent contribution to their income. Some will indeed then start performing to the camera which can make the result appear contrived and posey; it's better to let them settle down to their act and then sneak pictures without their knowing. They are easy subjects to photograph unless they are moving rapidly in poor light, when you really start to appreciate a camera with auto focusing and a large aperture lens. The more interesting and colourful ones work the theatre queues which in winter means working by flash or preferably by the existing street lighting; the youngsters who play musical instruments in the Underground, often remarkably well, don't usually make worthwhile pictures on their own. However if you can include the hurrying passengers or find a worthwhile setting it's worth having a go.

There is always a market for eye-catching industrial pictures, in this case a load of rock being tipped into a giant stone crusher. Since part of the subject was in heavy shadow and part in brilliant sunlight I had to use a powerful flash to try to even up the lighting, the synchronising speed of 1/60th giving a certain amount of blur to the falling rocks. An 18mm super wide lens exaggerated the size of the crusher in relation to the lorry and the man. You must of course get permission for this type of work, which has its dangers, must know what you are doing and how close it is safe to stand, and must be equipped with a hard hat. Above all you must avoid interfering with the work or making a nuisance of yourself—industrial work is rather specialised and needs experience.

extraordinary experience to explore the centre of a city at, say, 5.30 on a sunny morning, first having worked out a list of interesting eastward-facing architecture—though the early morning light will show up lots of other subjects which you have never previously considered.

A river curving through a town is always worth following. In London, for instance, if you walk in the early morning along the South Bank (which actually faces due West), for an hour or two the buildings on the opposite side of the river stand out in a magical manner; in the late evening you can take similar pictures from the North bank. This is one of the occasions when a zoom lens is especially useful since there is little you can do to alter the distance between you and the subject.

Working in the streets, a wide angle lens will be almost essential, avoiding converging verticals by the techniques already discussed. If, however, you want to photograph the skyscrapers with which so many cities decorate their centres it may well be impossible to include the tops without tilting. In this case tilt very boldly so that the convergence is obvious and dramatic, adding to the impression of height.

If you live in one of the tourist towns—Edinburgh, Stratford, Oxford, London or Canterbury for example—it is no exaggeration to say that they have probably been photographed millions of times. Luckily for us, only a tiny proportion of the results would be of much interest to people other than the photographers concerned, and an experienced worker who concentrates hard can always find a new way in which to take something as obvious as the Tower of London or the Houses of Parliament. Don't ignore such subjects because they have been overdone in the past; there is a steady demand for unfamiliar views of familiar subjects.

Since you live on the spot you can always take the pictures in the best possible lighting conditions; you have, or should have, local contacts; and you may well be able to make use of other buildings from which to take the photographs. Exploit the advantages of dwelling in the town to the full.

Night photography can often turn a boring building into something strange and fascinating. Floodlighting alone is not usually very exciting but can become so if an interesting foreground is included. Exposures will probably be around one or two seconds at f8 with a medium speed film, so a sturdy tripod will be needed. More atmospheric results are obtained by using the ordinary existing street lighting, taking care not to include a source of light such as a lamppost in the picture since it will produce flare—find a camera position from which the light is masked by a tree, the angle of a building or some similar object. If the pavements are wet after rain the reflections will add to the interest and since the exposure may run into minutes, depending on the power of the lighting, a watch must be kept for passing cars since their headlights would cause streaks across the picture. As soon as you hear a car approaching cover the lens with a piece of card or some similar opaque object until it has passed. The exposure is not at all critical; giving five or six minutes instead of one simply produces more shadow detail.

Perhaps the most interesting night pictures are taken at dusk in winter when the windows in shops and offices as well as the street lamps are lit up, but enough light is still left in the sky to show the clouds. Exposure is tricky since the balance between the sky and the streets will change quickly, and it is wise to bracket. Misty or foggy conditions can also transform prosaic scenes when heavy enough to cause lights to be turned on.

These days handheld night photography, thanks to the high speed films available, is technically fairly simple. With a lens that gives reasonable definition at a large aperture, f1.8 or f1.4, and a 1600 ASA emulsion (perhaps pushed to achieve this speed) it is almost true to say you can photograph anything you can see. The problem is, as always, to find something to interest other people. There is little point for instance in photographing the over-familiar neon signs in Piccadilly Circus when you can lower your camera and record the human curiosities around the base of Eros. It is an odd fact that though documentary night pictures can now be taken by almost anyone with a 35mm camera, very few technically perfect, visually interesting and saleable ones appear. Yet in the days of *Picture Post* some thirty years ago the staff, using comparatively slow film and cameras that are now collectors' items, produced a flow of memorable work.

Many amateurs feel shy about photographing strangers and never attempt this branch of documentary work, but if you are under contract to supply such pictures for a book or have been asked (ordered) to do so by an editor it is surprising how quickly all your inhibitions disappear. There is no spur like necessity and the professional knows that if he doesn't produce the goods he won't eat; the amateur on the other hand has a choice and tends to choose subjects with no danger of embarrassment. Once you have exposed a few cassettes on unknown people, day or night, you will lose any shyness and will have gone a long way towards becoming an efficient recorder of the British scene.

It is always wise if you can to include some indication of the place you are photographing—this is a very obvious example. Cardinal Cap Alley, next door to the house in which it is mistakenly said that Christopher Wren lived while St. Paul's was being rebuilt, is so narrow that you can brace your elbows against the wall on either side, eliminating camera shake even though you are using a small stop to obtain maximum depth of field. The temptation is to use a wide angle lens, but if you do the Cathedral will appear too small and distant.

Taking pictures for an article on Smithfield Meat Market I had to work early in the morning since everything quietens down after 9 a.m. The porters (called bummarees) are for some reason or other none too keen on being photographed, so it was necessary to work quickly and quietly. I wanted a shot of them relaxing so I fitted a 100 mm lens and strolled along the opposite side of the road, first carefully focusing on something that was the same distance away as the porters would be when I came opposite them. As soon as I reached the right position I took the camera from under my jacket, composed the picture and pressed the release without pausing for, at most, a couple of seconds; I doubt if anyone realised he had been photographed.
Using a shutter speed of 1/500th to avoid the chance of camera shake, a stop of f5.6 gave remarkable sharpness. Though the camera was my vintage XE1, the lens was a modern Minolta which has greater contrast and higher definition than the previous Rokkor type. Fitting a modern lens to an old body can often result in a surprising improvement in quality.

A Day's Work

To give you a better idea of what is involved in producing pictures of Britain for profit, let's take just one day. It is not typical since no two days are alike (for me this is one of the main appeals of photography) but may represent the kind of thing you will find yourself doing from time to time.

I had been asked to supply a selection of up to date colour and black and white pictures for a book on Kent. The printing schedule had been unexpectedly advanced and they were needed in a hurry, so I would have to cram as much work into the day as possible. From the point of view of getting the best possible results this is the wrong approach but I'm afraid it happens often enough in the hard commercial world.

The day before I have checked the car and filled it with petrol (few things are more annoying than to have to stop work and search for a filling station), prepared some food and put in the fridge, checked the equipment, films and the weather forecast, memorised routes by studying maps and made a list in the correct order of the places I intended to visit and the subjects I hoped to take.

Rising early, I left my home in North West London at 5.30 a.m. on a late spring morning with the sun just above the horizon, and threaded my way through the deserted streets towards the Blackwall Tunnel, being careful to keep to the speed limit since at this hour bored policemen welcome any diversion. Even so, it's astonishing how quickly you can cross a big town if there is no traffic.

The M20 was quickly reached and I was at my first objective, the village of Leeds, around 6.30. Parking the car near the Norman church I followed a footpath East towards Battel Hall, early 14th century, one of the many "oldest inhabited houses in England" and certainly worth recording. However, the front was closely enclosed in shadow and almost impossible to photograph. Would it be possible to take a picture from a distance showing it set in its surroundings, a technique I have often used with tricky subjects?

Luck, as necessary to a photographer as a camera, was with me. Walking past the house I found a field full of sheep and lambs, making an ideal foreground, and a tall tree to frame the pastoral scene. The soft sunlight came from exactly the right direction. I opened the gadget bag for the first picture of the day, hanging the two camera bodies on different lengths of strap round my neck. A 24 mm lens exaggerated the perspective and gave depth to the picture.

The footpath now led me to a distant view of Leeds Castle. I was facing into the light

I had been photographing in Chichester and had returned to the car park when glancing up I saw the sun just above the spire of the Cathedral. Stopping down to f16 and setting the shutter at 1/1000th I obtained a silhouette, knowing from previous experience that a pattern of rays would result. Nearly all lenses, with a few honourable exceptions, produce such a pattern when pointed at a very bright source of light and once you know the effect it can be turned to advantage. Straightforward, conventional pictures of well-known buildings hardly ever appeal to editors—you have to turn out something they haven't seen before.

The appeal of this picture of the entrance to Smarden Church, Kent, depends almost entirely on the bicycle, left there by a lady who was doing some flower-arranging inside. Though shooting directly into the sun, the top of the lychgate acted as a giant lenshood while the brightly-lit flagstones reflected a soft light into the shadows. I feel it would be a mistake to include a person in a picture like this since the bicycle says it all; keep a look out for similar objects you can include which convey an atmosphere. When making the print the flagstones had to be burnt in a little since the range of tones was too great for the paper.

Every summer tourists with their cameras crowd the narrow main street of Bosham in Sussex, trying to photograph the village. It's extremely difficult to get a good general view but it should be obvious that by moving to the other side of the inlet, a five minute walk, not only would there be no difficulty but the light would come from the right direction—no one does so. Whenever I have moved with relief from the busy village to the far side of the water I have had the whole place to myself. In order to include a large area of Sussex sky I used a 35 mm lens and added an orange filter, making a base of the buildings. This type of subject calls for a medium speed or, preferably, a slow film since broad areas of even tone such as the clouds will show the grain structure. Subjects with a lot of bold, contrasty detail will have the opposite effect; grain will not be obvious even with a fast film provided the picture is really sharp.

and knew that back-lit landscapes rarely sell, but the scene was so like an 18th century engraving, with cattle and sheep so perfectly positioned that I had to photograph it, trusting to the slight morning mist to diffuse some of the light into the shadows and using a 100 mm lens to increase the size of the castle in relation to that of the cattle. It was a picture that would have to be retaken in the late evening next time I was in the area but it is always worth having a go even if conditions are not ideal (and it was actually used).

So far I hadn't seen a living soul and the whole area was so beautiful that the temptation arose to spend more time just strolling around seeing what subjects turned up, but this attitude to work is fatal and should be reserved for the holidays. So it was back to the car and on to the large, cheerful village of Lenham. By now the road towards London was becoming busy with commuters but driving East was still easy.

There was plenty of parking space in the big square and I was taking pictures of my first subject, a chemist's shop, by 8.30. Why a chemist's shop? Well, it is called the "Saxon Warrior" because when it was being restored the body of a Saxon was found buried under one corner. It is a fine example of a mediaeval Wealden house and together with its name and the story made a useful item to add to the collection. Then on to the great Tithe Barn (a replacement for ones burnt together with the church in 1295 by someone who didn't like paying taxes to the clergy) and by using the 24 mm lens I could include the barn, the church and some blossom—in Kent in spring you'd have to, wouldn't you?

Back in the Square the shops were starting to open and once again there was the temptation to stay and photograph the good people of Lenham gossiping under the lime trees, the ancient pubs, the flagstone pavements and all the things that might have made pictures, but I was working to a tight schedule, trying to take subjects that I had previously researched and which I knew would sell.

A few miles along the new busy road brought me to Charing where I parked the car beside the ruins of the Archbishop's Palace, a victim of the Reformation and now a farm standing beside the church. Inside the ancient walls that surround the farm stands the Banqueting Hall, today used as a huge barn, in which Henry VIII and 4000 of his retainers ate on their way to the Field of the Cloth of Gold. I wanted to include it in a picture of the part-palace, part-farmhouse and the only way to do this without trespassing (why make photographers unpopular?) was to use my invaluable 17 mm lens. While fitting it, a man with a pick digging a hole by the entrance gate asked me what was the focal length of the lens, did it give distortion, etc.—everyone's a photographer these days!

A few more pictures of the church and its odd surroundings were taken with the 24 mm and then in the High Street I photographed the oldest butcher's shop in Britain—and while doing so a street-sweeper started a discussion about the merits of the 5″ × 4″ Speed Graphics we used to use. Such talks are never time-wasting since you can gain from them invaluable local knowledge.

So far I had been driving in an almost straight line, but I felt a four mile diversion south to Pluckley was justified. Pluckley happens to be the most haunted village in England, boasting some dozen ghosts at the most recent count, but I was there to record the round-topped "Dering Windows" installed in all the local houses, shops, the school and the inn by a 19th century squire who thought they were lucky. While taking the good example over the butcher's shop the owner came out and said there were some fine views of the Weald to be taken from a ridge a short distance away. I followed his advice and was rewarded with what in clear weather must be a superb scene—but the distance was

It would be interesting to know how many of the literally millions of pictures taken of the Cutty Sark were saleable. Editors dismiss conventional pictures at once since they have seen them all before so to get something different the 15mm Hologon was brought into action. Having found an interesting angle time was needed before the two children wandered into the right position to give a centre of interest and a sense of scale. At the fixed stop of f8 a shutter speed of 1/250th was needed on FP4.

Throwley Church lies in a remarkably quiet, remote part of Kent—I have sat for an hour on the verge of the lane that leads to it and the only passing traffic was a woman on a bicycle. Wondering how to convey this sense of tranquility I walked through the fields surrounding the building and came across the horse happily grazing. With practice you don't compose pictures consciously, instead you move around until the elements are more or less in the right place without thinking about it. There was little subject movement so with the metering system set on automatic I selected a shutter speed that would give me a small stop and plenty of depth.

diffused by a haze. Never mind, I took pictures anyway with the inevitable sheep, lambs and trees in the foreground, resolving to return on one of those crisp days you get after stormy weather when you can see to infinity.

Back to Charing and, first looking at the map, on to remote Throwley Forstal, an almost unspoilt example of the way villages in Kent appeared fifty years ago. The little Post Office in a timber-framed house, the barn on the edge of the green, the colour-washed cottages, the pefect pub—I had listed no special subjects and just wandered round trying to record the tranquillity, no easy thing to do with a camera.

The nearby hamlet of Throwley has a surprising church full of surprising monuments. I was after the statue of the Lord Harris who watched an operation on his own brain, but first I took an exterior of the church with a horse grazing in the foreground to convey the atmosphere of the place. Traffic roars along the motorways to the North and South in a continuous stream, leaving the area in between deserted—while taking a break and some food before tackling the monuments the only person or vehicle I saw was a woman on a bicycle.

The Harris monument was photographed with a 50 mm lens and two small flash units I had been carrying in the boot (no point in adding to the weight of the gadget bag), one fitted with a slave unit, the other with an extension lead. Then I turned to the extraordinary Sondes memorials in which a man and a woman, crudely carved and highly coloured, kneel facing each other. The shortage of space called for the 17 mm lens and since the light was poor, the invaluable monopod.

Then North to Faversham. There was a market taking place, the same market that Shakespeare saw when he visited the town as a strolling player, but this wasn't due to luck—I had chosen a market day for my visit. Back in London I had decided it was essential to photograph Faversham Creek with its odd assortment of boats and also Arden's House in Abbey Street (the mayor, he was murdered there in 1576), and having polished these off I was free to concentrate on the market and its traders, using 100 and 50 mm lenses. You can't plan this sort of photography ahead, and the danger is that it can become so interesting that you spend the rest of the day and most of your film on the various characters you encounter.

It was very difficult indeed to leave Faversham but the early start to the day was beginning to tell and once you lose your enthusiasm it's time to stop. I had researched enough subjects to last until sunset and was only halfway through the list, but decided to tackle the remainder on another day, starting out in the early afternoon.

However, while I was in the area I thought I'd take one last subject—the secluded Norton church approached through an orchard. The blossom would be out and judging by the map the light would be coming from the right direction. After getting lost in the lanes I finally found it and used the 100 mm lens to compress the long length of blossom-laden trees and increase the size of the church in the background. Then back to London, just missing the rush hour surge.

The point to note is that a list of sure-fire subjects—"bankers" if you like—had been prepared beforehand in the right order so that as little travelling as possible was involved. All possible information about them had been collected and study of the map had indicated the best camera positions. Other unexpected subjects had of course been taken as they appeared, but I had to be sure that the day would produce enough publishable pictures to justify the expense.

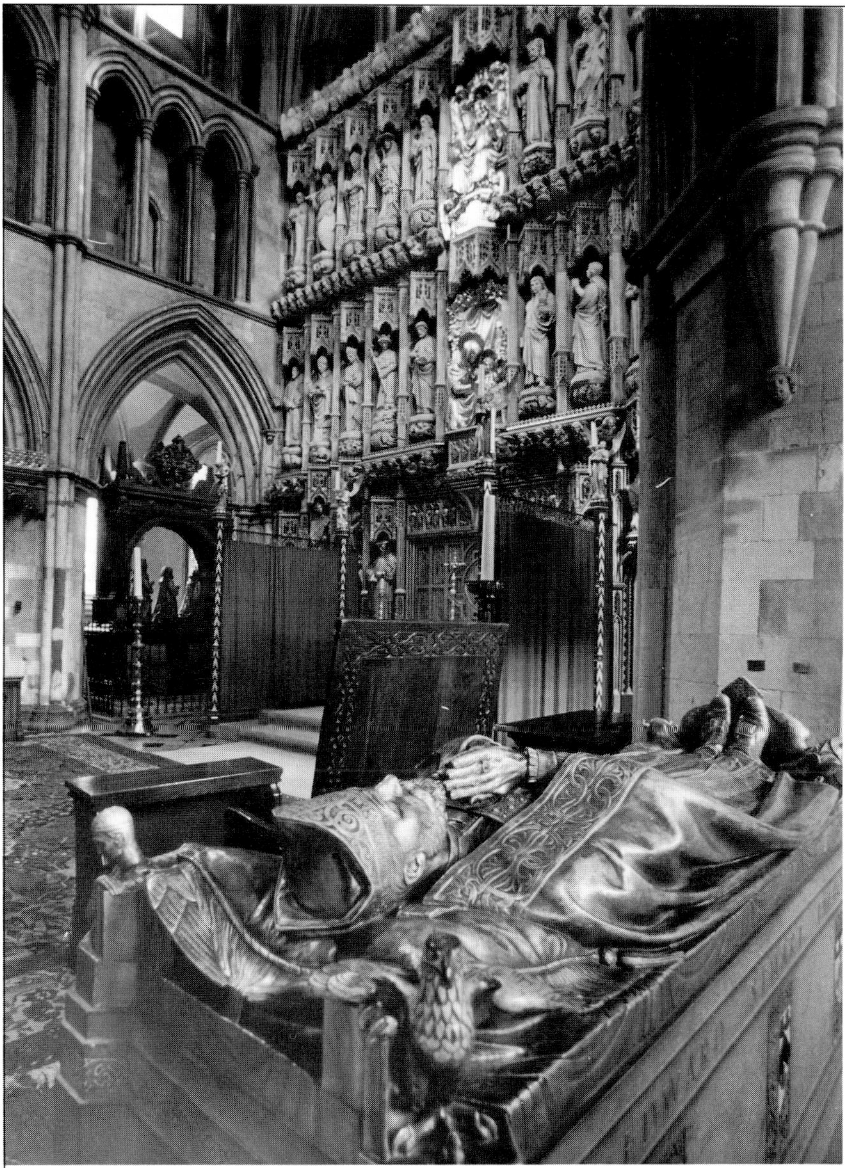

Though Southwark Cathedral is unique and fascinating it is, thank Heaven, comparatively neglected by the tourists. The 17 mm lens I used for this picture was set at open aperture, f2.8, but even so the depth of field was reasonably good. The only problem was to keep the camera steady for the $\frac{1}{2}$ second exposure needed so I pressed it hard against a convenient pillar; provided the support is really solid and steady exposures of several seconds duration can be made in this way.

It is also worth mentioning that as soon as taking photographs becomes drudgery instead of being a pleasure, in other words when you become tired, it is time to stop. Successful pictures are the ones you enjoy taking.

Let me repeat, this was not a typical day. If covering important towns such as Canterbury or Rochester you would have to spend as much time in them as could be economically justified and if not under financial or deadline pressure it would be wise (and very pleasant) to spend a whole morning or afternoon in the larger villages so as to photograph them more fully and discover new subject matter. Adjust the time you spend on your photography to suit the circumstances.

The lily-filled moat at Hever isn't really all that wide but I wanted it to form both a base and a lead-in to the Castle, which was flatly lit since the day had become overcast. By positioning the 15mm Hologon near the edge of the water the leaves of the lilies seemed to move towards the house and add some feeling of action to an otherwise static subject. The view through the finder was completely different to that seen by the eye, which could only include a limited amount of the scene—you need a lot of practice before you really feel at home with a super wide.

Part of a subject often makes a better picture than the whole. This 1916 Sopwith Pup, one of the most pleasant planes to fly ever designed, is powered by an 80 h.p. Gnome rotary engine that spins at the same rate as the airscrew. In order to give an idea of the movement I used a shutter speed of 1/30th to produce blur—a faster speed might have frozen the engine and given a static result. A low camera angle increased the apparent size and importance of the plane. It was taken at a private air display; you cannot usually get close to the flying aircraft at the public ones.

For most of the day the ancient Downland figure of the Long Man of Wilmington is in the shade and the problem is to get a picture with enough contrast to reproduce well. I got far enough away to include some of the surroundings and used an orange filter. Then when I came to make the print I used an extra hard paper to obtain a bold result from a flat subject, a common technique with dull landscapes. To sell a picture like this it should be accompanied by plenty of information, preferably in the form of an article. Is the figure Celtic, Roman, cut by mediaeval monks from the nearby priory, an 18th century joke? No one knows and you can form your own theory. I'm pretty sure it is Celtic but that originally it looked very different, but whatever you think there's lots of material for a short, readable article.

Processing and Printing

In the chapter on "Which Film?" we have already mentioned that the home-processing of E6 film is really only justified if you like doing it and that you should instead make use of a good, professional laboratory that will produce results in a couple of hours if necessary, increase or decrease the speed of your film at no extra cost, mount your 35 mm transparencies and treat your work with care.

However for much of your photography of Britain there will be no great rush to see the results and there is no reason why you should not use the process-paid Kodachrome which many editors prefer for 35 mm work (some actually insist on it) and which has non-fading dyes. Apart from the satisfaction of craftsmanship there is little virtue in processing your own colour.

The situation regarding black and white processing is completely different. Due to the time and skill required, to have your films processed and printed by a laboratory is very expensive and, no matter how eminent and experienced the printer, you always have the feeling you could have done slightly better yourself. Newspapers and magazines usually employ staff to handle processing and printing, using their photographers solely to take pictures, but freelances must keep down their overheads and make their own prints which is much more satisfactory in every way.

If you have so far been taking pictures for your own pleasure or for the admiration of your friends it may come as a shock to know that in the commercial world an editor has not the slightest interest in the camera, lens or film you used or in the skill that was needed to take the picture; the only thing that matters to him is the print on his desk. If it has impact and is of good quality he will consider it but if not it will be discarded.

Many photographers would be surprised and hurt if they knew how briefly the picture editor of a national newspaper examines their work. He sees many hundreds of prints every day, he knows exactly what will catch the eye of the reader and can sum up the quality of your work immediately. You have only a matter of seconds in which to capture his attention so your print must be boldly composed and have a range of tones stretching from the maximum black of the paper to a clear highlight; there is no time in which to appreciate the subtleties of tone or content. The printing of most of today's papers is so poor that they would be lost anyway.

Magazines and books are better able to reproduce tones and fine detail, and compositions do not have to be so obvious, but you must still make use of the full range of

When using black and white material the traditional advice is to "expose for the shadows and develop for the highlights" but sometimes a silhouette with hardly any shadow detail at all can be more effective than a picture with a normal range of tones. In this case had the correct exposure been given for the shadows all detail in the hazy background would have been burnt out and lost, and the result would have lacked impact. Exposing for this type of subject is a tricky business and it is wise to bracket, especially when shooting colour.

While photographing the Royal Observatory at Herstmonceux the old ghost story of the giant Phantom Drummer who strides along the battlements beating his drum cropped up. I mentioned innocently to one of the astronomers that I'd never seen a picture of the ghost's path and since he never had either we climbed up to the roof. The ghost didn't oblige but I took this unique picture of his beat; the weather was dull so I printed it on the hardest grade of paper and held back the path with the shadow of a pencil to lighten it and make it stand out boldly.

the printing paper. Inexperienced photographers sometimes think that this means making contrasty prints but this is a fundamental error. When a photograph is reproduced there is inevitably a slight compression of the tone range and if your print is harsh to start with it will be even harsher on the printed page. The object is to make prints with a good black in the densest shadows and with sparkling highlights, but with the fullest possible range of tones in between.

This starts with the negative and its development. It is impossible to over-stress the importance of choosing a good, standard negative developer made by some well-known manufacturer and of using it until you have learnt how to get exactly the result you want. For over sixty years the most-used fine grain developer was M.Q.-Borax (Kodak's D76 or Ilford's ID11) which still gives a very good compromise between grain, speed and sharpness but is inconvenient to use in small volumes—say 600 ml. For each successive film developed the time has to be increased slightly if contrast is to remain the same and a record has to be kept of the number of films processed. A better method is to make up a much larger volume, perhaps 4 or 5 litres, drawing off the amount needed to fill the tank and tipping it back after use; the change in contrast will be so slight as not to matter for a long time. Some workers take half the volume needed and dilute it with an equal quantity of water, throwing it away after use, but this can become an expensive way of working.

To overcome this problem concentrated developers were introduced, a small volume being greatly diluted and then discarded, the theory being that each film is processed in fresh developer. This works well provided you use up the entire contents of the bottle in a reasonable time; if a quarter-full bottle is left on the shelf for months the contents will deteriorate. An exception, recommended to photographers who only process occasionally, is Ilford's "Ilfotech LC29", a highly concentrated solution which seems to last in the bottle indefinitely.

Broadly speaking, concentrated developers can be divided into two groups, those which apparently increase the definition of the film by giving increased sharpness to the edges of objects (increasing the sharpness of the grain at the same time), and those which give a slightly smeary grain structure, making it less visible. Paterson's "Acutol" is a good example of the former and "Aculux" of the latter. Most people prefer to use the "high definition" developers with slow and medium speed films in which the grain is fine to start with. The ones that produce a less visible grain structure are ideal for fast films, though if your subjects have large areas of smooth tones, clouds for instance, which show up grain in a marked manner, there is a lot to be said for using a medium speed film in a grain-reducing developer.

Developers are also available which will give reasonable results if you have been forced to under expose by up to a couple of stops, but they are not recommended for normal use since they inevitably increase grain.

Whichever film/developer combination you choose, start off by following the manufacturer's instructions to the letter. These days most seem to presume you will be printing the negatives with a diffusion enlarger which needs a higher negative contrast than the condenser variety but there is little standardisation, any more than there is with paper manufacturer's idea of what is a "normal" grade. In addition variations will be introduced by the accuracy of your thermometer, your ability to measure small volumes of concentrated developer, your form of agitation and even the make of tank you are using. With luck if you follow the instructions all will go well, but you may have to adjust the development time to suit your particular technique and equipment. Once you have arrived at the correct figure you can standardise your negative contrast and printing becomes much more simple.

For a long time there was a common photographic notion that condenser enlargers gave greater sharpness than the diffuser type, but very careful tests have shown that the only difference is one of contrast. Flat prints never appear as sharp as contrasty ones and diffusion lighting lowers the contrast by about one grade of paper. Provided you adjust for this, either by using a harder grade or preferably by adjusting the development time of the film, you will see no difference in the results.

I prefer diffuser enlargers, in other words ones with "colour heads", for black and white work because they keep spotting to a minimum. Using a Durst 605 I have a piece of glass in the upper part of the negative carrier but have replaced the lower one with a glassless frame, reducing the possible dust-attracting surfaces by two. Replacing the top glass by a second metal frame will reduce the chance of dust still further, but if you are making a number of prints from the same negative the heat may cause it to curl slightly, making constant refocusing necessary. The upper sheet of glass prevents this upwards curl and with normal care you will not have to do any spotting at all. You should, of course, never submit prints with dust spots to an editor since it looks so careless and unprofessional.

Right from the start you should standardise on a print size, 10″ × 8″ being usual. Some workers like to submit 12″ × 9½″ ones because they appear more impressive, but they may not fit into a filing system, need special envelopes and are more expensive to post (posting will be an important overhead and must be kept to a minimum). Borderless 10″ × 8″ prints look surprisingly larger than similar ones with a border but the paper easel required may not be as easy to use as the normal type.

It is worth mentioning that these days there is no point at all in using a hardening fixer for either films or paper, which have been prehardened during manufacture. All it will do is to greatly lengthen the washing time which will otherwise be very short in the case of films and a resin-coated paper. The traditional fibre-based paper is still needed if you are making "archival quality" prints that have to last indefinitely but is unnecessary for ordinary work. Try to keep printing and processing as simple and as rapid as possible.

I use "variable contrast" paper to avoid stockkeeping problems, adjusting the grade by means of the colour head. Though an enlarging exposure meter will give you a good approximation of the correct print exposure, a test strip will be more accurate and will give you more information.

Since all competent photographers know how to print successfully there is no point in going into details in this book, but it may be worth mentioning that some people try to economise by purchasing an inexpensive enlarging lens. All the time and money that has been invested in the camera, the taking of the picture and the processing of the film will be wasted unless the enlarging lens is at least up to the standard of the one on the camera. The sharpness, contrast and especially the covering power given by an enlarging lens of good quality will come as a revelation if you have so far used an inferior one, but unless it is kept clean and free from dust and damp the performance will soon fall off. After every printing session I remove mine from the enlarger and store it in its original dust-proof container to protect it from stop-bath and fixer fumes.

Weak skys will be lost in reproduction so as often as not some "printing-in" will be needed to give them strength. Foregrounds may have to be held back to reveal detail, small too-light areas burnt in—in short you will need all your printing skills to produce a print that will have impact and at the same time reproduce well—not necessarily the same thing. Many books have been published on printing technique but there is no substitute for experience; no matter how long you have been in the game you gain in skill with every print you make.

You can be quite sure that every windmill you see has been photographed many times over but they are still irresistible subjects. Instead of taking a straightforward record it is wise to either get well back and include the surroundings or else to get close and concentrate on bold detail. Here a 24 mm lens was used to emphasise the fantail, an orange filter darkened the sky and a figure was included to give a sense of scale—though small it plays an important part in the composition.

We had been taking publicity pictures for Guinness of their hop harvest when it started to drizzle, so we instead explored the country round Bodiam Castle. Climbing the footpath that leads up the hill behind the building we were able to look down on it, an unusual view that few people record because in normal weather you are looking straight into the sun. The dull weather, however, made the sun invisible so apart from the flat lighting and lack of contrast there was no problem. An 85mm lens compressed the perspective slightly but a stop of f11 was needed to obtain sufficient depth of field. This in turn called for a shutter speed of 1/60th so I braced myself against a tree and hoped there wouldn't be any camera shake. Incidentally if you are taking pictures in the rain a really deep lenshood is essential.

I used to wonder how the Victorian photographers of East Anglia, Emerson in particular, obtained such magnificently soft, subtly-lit results. Did they use some secret or perhaps a special developer? Was it their printing technique? Then I spent some time there and realised it was all due to the natural lighting; the enormous spread of sky and the flat landscape makes you feel you are working inside a huge matte reflector, the light reaching everywhere. Walberswick Ferry in Suffolk was taken on an overcast but luminous day with a 35 mm lens, the quality of the light being quite unlike that in any other part of Britain. You wouldn't think such a small island could have such a variety of light but each area is unique—why do photographers ever want to go abroad?

Corfe Castle in Dorset makes a worthwhile picture from many angles, but I wanted to show it in relation to the village. Getting well back and climbing a bank it was possible to make a foreground of the ancient Greyhound Inn but it meant shooting almost into the light. However, it helped to show the uneven pattern of the roof tiles and was perhaps better than having the light coming from a more conventional angle. Enough exposure had to be given to record the shadow detail and an "averaging" meter system would have been over-affected by the sky. "Centre-weighted" or "spot" metering copes well with this type of subject.

Presentation

The way in which you present your work to the potential buyer can make all the difference between a sale and a rejection. You want to convey an impression of professionalism and efficiency and nothing destroys this more quickly than sloppy display. It is not unusual for an editor to receive a packet of prints of widely differing sizes and surfaces, some perhaps mounted 15″ × 12″ which the photographer made for an exhibition, a few 12″ × 9½″, some 10″ × 8″ and a handful of 7″ × 5″. The collection appears so careless and amateurish that it is usually rejected out of hand. In the same infuriating way he will be sent colour transparencies stacked together in the plastic box in which they were returned from the processor or, even worse, mounted in glass which will have to be removed before the slide can be reproduced and which may well crack in the post.

As has been mentioned in the chapter on processing, it is wise to standardise on a print size of 10″ × 8″ with, of course, a glossy surface. This will fit everyone's filing system, which a larger size may not, and if a borderless easel is used the prints will appear bigger than they really are. Every print must carry your name, address and phone number, and don't forget that the ink used in many pens and stamp pads rubs off resin-coated paper and the kind made specially to suit the material must be used.

Alternatively, printed self-adhesive labels can be used, or you can type the information on a sheet of paper and attach it with adhesive tape. 35 mm colour transparencies must be submitted in plastic filing sheets holding perhaps fifteen or sixteen slides, preferably with a matt backing. This allows them to be easily examined and compared either on a "light box" or by holding them up to a window. Medium format transparencies can be displayed in the same way, though some people prefer to place them individually in separate transparent envelopes.

Each slide should carry your name and address. There is no room for a proper caption, though the name of the location should be added for identification (see "Captions"). They should naturally all be inserted in the filing sheet the correct way round for viewing, emulsion side down.

Prints and especially slides are valuable and must be properly packed for the post. When packing prints, ordinary stiffened manilla envelopes do not really give enough protection and it is wise to include a sheet of heavy board that won't bend easily and which just fits into the envelope—thin card or corrugated paper is useless. If using unstiffened envelopes make sure they are made from really tough paper and sandwich the prints between two sheets of close-fitting heavy board. Sheets of slides should be packed in the same way. Add a folded second envelope, stamped and addressed, for their return.

Look up the name of the editor or picture editor of the journal or publisher and address the package to him personally together with a short note describing the subject matter, the number of prints or slides submitted and the fact that you have enclosed a stamped, addressed envelope for their return. Don't go into long-winded details about the contents, yourself or the way in which the pictures were taken and never say how much you expect if they are published!

Captions

You have returned from a day's photography with clear memories of what you have taken, your colour material has been sent away for processing and you settle down to developing and printing your black and white work. A week later you start to caption the results, but was that village North Marden or East Marden? Was the church St Michael's or St Mary's? Where did you photograph that wheelwright? It was all so clear and obvious at the time but a week is quite long enough for you to forget the details.

There is really no alternative to writing down brief details of the location of each subject, the date and any information you have about it as soon as possible after taking the picture. It's a chore and the temptation is to tell yourself that you'll do it when you get home, but you won't. Accurate captions are so vital to picture sales that many photographers carry cards in their gadget bags with the numbers 1 to 36 printed down one side and a space opposite every number in which to write the details. Of course one caption will often cover a number of pictures of the same subject but you must be able to caption individual frames if necessary.

When you come to expand your notes, put yourself in the place of the picture editor. A caption such as "A Sussex Village" or "The Old Barn" is meaningless. He wants to know exactly where the picture was taken and have all the information you can give him about the place. If necessary he can cut it down.

Never give information that the viewer can gain for himself from the picture. "Building a Dry-stone Wall" is useless, but "Charlie Butts aged 80 has been building drystone walls around Painswick in the Cotswolds for the last sixty-five years as did his father and grandfather before him. The technique is unchanged since the Middle Ages" tells you something you can't see and helps to sell the photograph.

Keep a record of the date on which you took the picture but don't add it to the caption. A picture taken twenty years ago can still sell perfectly well but if the editor sees when it was taken he may well be prejudiced against it. Old Kodachromes which are date-stamped should have a self-adhesive label giving your name and address placed over the date—no one is going to bother peeling it off! It is of course essential that all your pictures carry your name, address and phone number, as has already been mentioned, even if your captions are written on a separate sheet.

When submitting a variety of black and white prints the captions will normally be typed on sheets of paper which are fixed to the back with adhesive tape. However, if you are submitting a large number of pictures to illustrate a book or a magazine article many editors prefer you to write an identification number or letter on the back of the print with the corresponding captions written separately. It gives more room for information and makes things easier for the typesetter. With colour, of course, this method is essential.

Writing An Article

Many pictures are unsaleable unless accompanied by a short, interesting article. Few journals, for instance, would buy a picture of an East End doss-house but if it is backed up by an account of how Stalin and Litvinov stayed there in 1907 it immediately becomes important. Your information would come from general reading and research, and having located the place and taken the picture you would then write the article. However, for many photographers this is the stumbling block, since they feel it is beyond them and should be left to the professionals. In fact, though, most people can write in an interesting and readable way provided they tell a plain story in a simple fashion, just as though they were talking to a friend.

The rules are simple. Don't use a long word or phrase if a short one will convey the same meaning; "bad weather" is better than "unfavourable climatic conditions". Vary the length of your sentences and paragraphs but keep them fairly short since readers don't like to be faced by a mass of uninterrupted typematter. Never try to show how clever or well-educated you are and never be condescending or write down to your readers.

Try to capture attention right from the start by giving some interesting or little-known information. In the case of the subject previously mentioned, the article could begin "When Stalin, the ruler of Russia, was in the East End he stayed in a doss-house in Fieldgate Street; Litvinov, later Ambassador to the United States, slept in the next cubicle. Tower House miraculously escaped the Blitz and is as busy today as it was in 1907, etc, etc.".

A picture of horses grazing in a field in Kent would rarely interest an editor on its own, but if he read in an accompanying article that it showed the spot where Jack Cade, leader of the 1450 rebellion, was killed by the Sheriff of Kent under highly suspicious circumstances, the picture and the article combine together to become worthwhile. Even a picture of the Stage Door at the Adelphi Theatre can be sold when the editor reads that this is where the actor William Terriss was murdered in 1897 and that his ghost still appears there and at Covent Garden Underground Station (another otherwise dull picture).

Photographers, like journalists, must acquire a surface knowledge of a vast variety of subjects—you cannot read too much or talk to too many people. Remember that an article not only sells otherwise unsaleable pictures but that the combination brings in many times more money than the pictures alone. In the same way that good photography is largely a matter of practice, so the more you write the easier it will become.

Articles should be typed with double-spacing, leaving room for the editor to make additions or alterations, and the pages should be numbered and clipped or stapled together. The first sheet should only carry the title, your name and address, the date and the approximate number of words. The amount of paperwork that lands on an editor's desk every day is staggering and if your article is not easily identifiable there is a good chance that it will be lost. Try to make things as easy as possible.

Don't expect your article and pictures to be published immediately. Every magazine and newspaper carries a reserve stock of material in their files to fill a space in an

Every spring at the Equinox the Druids, wearing robes designed by a 19th century German professor, climb Parliament Hill in North London to perform the necessary ceremonies—it has become so familiar that few professional photographers bother to turn up. However, every recorder of the English scene should have the Druids in his files and I took this from a low angle as they climbed the hill, including lots of sky to add to the atmosphere. Similar odd happenings take place all over Britain and since they usually occur at the same time and the same place, if you miss the show one year you can plan to photograph it on the next occasion.

emergency and your effort may be included with these. If for some reason or other it is unsuited to the style of the journal it will probably be returned without delay; if not it is probably being held for possible future use. It is of course unlikely that you will see your submission again unless a stamped, addressed envelope of the correct size is enclosed. This adds to your overheads, but prints are quite expensive to make while transparencies are irreplaceable, so both must be retrieved. Loss of the article itself is not so important since you will have the essential carbon copy in your own files.

Finally, if you really feel you haven't the time or ability to produce articles why not team up with someone who can write but can't take photos? By doing this you will both find it much easier to sell your material.

The Marketplace

There are thousands of skilful, intelligent amateur photographers who produce a constant flow of interesting, technically perfect pictures of Britain but whose work never appears in print. They may lack initiative, they may have been disheartened by a couple of refusals in the past or they may simply not want the bother of packing their work and hawking it round the picture market.

There are also smaller numbers of mediocre photographers who earn a steady income from their rather ordinary pictures because their real talent lies in studying the market closely and in knowing exactly who is likely to use their work. Usually extrovert, they are unaffected by refusals and are persistent and energetic.

Then there is the small lucky band who combine creative talent with a gift for salesmanship. The qualities required are very different and it is unusual for them to be found in the same person. Photographers who take pictures of places rather than of people tend to be rather shy and introverted. However for these people there is a solution—use an agency.

Agencies

A good agency can take all the drudgery out of selling your pictures, leaving you free to concentrate on producing a flow of saleable material. They will usually take 50% of the reproduction fee (some take 60% some 40%) and in return will reach sections of the market you would never think of approaching, especially overseas ones, will save you all the bother of packing and postage (an expensive overhead), will chase slow payers and will sell and resell your pictures over a period of years.

Before approaching an agency you must of course find out if they handle your type of material—ones that specialise in news pictures are unlikely to be interested in British landscapes. The first step is to study the requirements of the various agencies, very full details being given in the essential *Freelance Photographer's Market Handbook* and more briefly in *The Writers' and Artists' Yearbook*, another publication that should be always to hand. Then, having chosen a likely agency you must write asking if they are willing to take on a new photographer, be prepared to submit a first collection of perhaps at least 200 saleable slides which they will retain for from one to five years, and tell them approximately how many more pictures you expect to be able to send them each year.

These conditions may seem a bit stiff but they are quite logical. You may sell a picture once during the course of a year but the agency may sell it four times over the same period, giving you twice the return, so in spite of the commission you are better off. The cost of taking on a new photographer is high because a good deal of work and organisation is needed for each new client. They must have a good turnover and they cannot do this unless you send them a large number of good pictures to start the ball rolling. These will have to be retained for at least a year or two because it takes time to market your collection properly and they cannot always get material back from a publisher quickly. And don't forget the agencies like enthusiastic, hard-working photographers who will keep sending them fresh material so that they can keep approaching their potential customers.

Every slide you submit should first be checked with an ×8 magnifier for sharpness, must be tightly composed, have good colour saturation, be free from dirt or scratches, and above all be eye-catching and have impact. Some photographers make the fundamental error of trying to sell their best pictures themselves so as to get the full reproduction fee, looking on the agency as a dumping ground for slightly over or under exposed transparencies, ones with incorrect colour balance, ones that are not quite in focus or have slight camera shake—in short they hope that in some miraculous way the agency will be able to sell unsaleable pictures. They won't; all that will happen is that you will annoy both them and the potential purchasers.

A good agency will look after your interests, encourage and advise you and provide you with a steady income for many years, but in return you must work hard, sending them a constant supply of technically perfect, interesting and above all saleable material. Every picture must carry a brief, informative caption that the agency can include in their filing system—"Tenterden Railway, Kent" or "Walberswick Ferry, Suffolk" is enough—and it is quite possible that they will want to remount your slides in their own standardised mounts. Treat the agency as a helpful friend and always remember you are not doing them a favour by letting them market your work; it is they who are doing you a favour by taking you on.

Newspapers

As one would expect, newspapers mainly publish news pictures and only a few of the quality papers occasionally carry a "Beautiful Britain" landscape, usually taken by a staff photographer. However, it is still possible to place your work with the nationals if it carries some topical message.

If you hear rumours that a bypass cutting through unspoilt country may be built, take a boldly composed picture of the area and send it with the fullest possible details to a paper that has shown interest in preserving the environment. Alternatively, "before and after" photos of the effects of buildings and motorways can be of interest.

"Curiosities" are often saleable, but may be held in the files for a long time until a space has to be filled. It is, of course, pointless to submit pictures of events sufficiently interesting and well-known to attract press and agency photographers—no editor is going to waste money on buying a picture that can be supplied by his staff. However, if you can take an eye-catching picture of some ceremony or event too small and obscure to attract much outside attention you may stand a chance of publication provided it is sufficiently off-beat.

The freelance is much more likely to place his work in local papers, the snag being that some of the smaller ones pay very badly or not at all, being used to waiving a fee in return for publicising some happening. Dealing with these is a waste of time and money—concentrate instead on the papers with a wide circulation that pay standard rates. Their photographic staff may be very small and unable to cover everything that is happening in the area, so it is quite likely that you will be able to place pictures of the lesser known local events, and in addition landscapes showing the beauty of the surrounding countryside.

However, most photographers of Britain look on newspapers very much as a sideline and concentrate on the vast magazine market.

Magazines

At present the magazine world is in a state of turmoil with old-established ones disappearing or merging, new ones blossoming briefly before folding, editors being changed overnight. It is almost impossible for the freelance to keep track of all that has happened without a close study of the BFP *Market Newsletter*, which every month lets you know of the changes that have taken place and gives the addresses and the requirements of the new journals that have appeared. Used in conjunction with the *Market Handbook* it really is essential reading.

The many thousands of magazines that are published can be divided into two main groups, the entertainment and leisure ones that appear on the bookstalls and the trade and house magazines that are unknown to the general public but which often have big circulations and pay well. They represent half the picture market and details can be found in the *Market Handbook*.

Marketing a picture so as to get the maximum return calls for imagination and effort. As an example, let's suppose someone has found an Edwardian electric carriage at the back of an old barn. You photograph it by low evening sunlight, ideal for this type of subject because it accentuates detail and gives a feeling of nostalgia, and include the owner in the picture to give human interest. Possible users are the national and local press, the county magazine, the many motoring magazines, the electrical trade journals, the manufacturers of the motor and components (if they still exist) for use in their house journals and the "Tyres and Accessories" magazine if the tyres are still in place. Then when it has been restored you can repeat the process with "before and after" pictures.

Again, you have photographed an exposed section of a Roman road surfaced with iron slag from the Roman furnaces, using a wide angle lens from a low angle and getting close enough to show the shape and size of the fragments; a human figure in the background gives an idea of the scale. As before, low lighting will emphasise the texture. This picture could be offered to the local press, the county magazine, the historical and archaeological press, to outdoor and country magazines and to the trade ones devoted to engineering and road construction and iron and steel production. Careful study of the magazines listed in the *Market Handbook* will suggest other possible users provided you use your imagination.

A picture of the statue of Lord Harris who, shot in the head at the battle of Bunker's Hill in 1775 during the American War of Independence, had mirrors rigged round the operating table so that he could watch the removal of the bullet from his own brain might provide light relief in a medical journal, could sell to American historical magazines, to the local press, to county and country magazines and so on. Of course, without the story behind it no one is going to buy a straightforward picture of a statue, hence the importance of research.

It may not be worth dealing with some of the small-circulation journals aimed at the hobby and enthusiast public since they may depend to a large extent on pictures supplied free or for publication at a nominal sum. Many people simply want to see the photos they have taken to illustrate their hobby in print and are not interested in any return, but you always have to bear in mind your constant overheads—it is a sobering experience to sit down and work out just how much you must receive for a simple black and white picture before you start to break even.

The photographic press can provide a market for your pictures of Britain provided you can tie in some photographic angle. Perhaps you have a series of good landscapes taken with a lens that has a very long or a very short focal length, maybe some new type of film was used, they may all have been taken during storms or in the early morning—there should be some common photographic factor since straightforward landscapes are rarely interesting enough on their own to justify publication. They should of course be accompanied by a short, informative article so that the readers can add to their photographic knowledge and perhaps gain new ideas.

The magazine market is so vast that almost any picture with interest and impact can be placed. Once you have found by trial and error which ones pay a fair fee promptly you can build up a connection, sending them work regularly. Always remember that if you photograph and write about things that interest you the results will probably interest other people as well.

A point often overlooked by inexperienced photographers is that most magazines are finalised a long time before publication. It is no use your submitting May Blossom pictures in March or April or your snow pictures in November or December. Covers in particular are prepared a long time in advance so allow as much time as possible when sending in your seasonal pictures. Once your work starts to appear regularly and you get to know the editor and his staff, you will learn the dates of the deadlines and will have a better idea of when to send in material, but to start with be prepared to wait three or four months before it is published.

Book Illustration

No photographer ever became rich from illustrating books, but it is a branch of publishing that can add a useful amount to your income. Some publishers simply turn to the agencies for their pictures but the more enterprising ones are always interested in new and original sources. Firms producing travel and guide books in particular are constantly looking for up to date pictures of Britain since it is only too easy to include pictures of views and buildings that have disappeared years ago; townscapes can change their appearance in a matter of months.

It is very unlikely that a book publisher will want to use your material immediately, but he will certainly want to know what pictures you have in your collection and the kind of subject in which you specialise so that when an appropriate title comes along in the future he can approach you. The *Writers' and Artists' Yearbook* lists most British publishers together with a selection of overseas ones and gives details of their interests; some concentrate on historical matters, some on travel, some on architecture and so on. You

Try to photograph every odd tombstone you see, since a good collection can provide the basis for several illustrated articles. Strong side lighting was used for this one in Ayr, Scotland, in order to show the remarkable detail—it's no good photographing carving on a dull day or against the light—and the camera was positioned almost on the ground. The lower the camera angle the more impressive the subject appears.

must study their requirements carefully and prepare a selection of your best work (not too much; a dozen pictures will be quite sufficient) which you can send together with a list of subjects you have in stock and will be taking in the future. Include, of course, the usual stamped, addressed envelope for the return of the pictures.

Many thousands of books are published in Britain each year and every firm is looking for new and original subjects that will sell. To think of one is a much more difficult proposition than you might imagine—every possible topic seems to have been covered. However, you may be able to find something slightly off-beat that you could cover or perhaps think of a new approach to a familiar subject. All publishers are glad of suggestions, and if your idea is sufficiently worthwhile will be able to find a writer to supply the words while you supply the illustrations.

If you can write yourself so much the better. The commissioning editor will of course need some proof of your ability, usually in the form of previously published work, but if satisfied may give you a contract to provide both words and pictures. This should work well since you can combine photography with on-the-spot research.

However, it is only too easy to allow enthusiasm for a subject to blind you to the practical realities of covering it. A summer holiday may have convinced you that there is a market for a book on The Fishing Villages of Cornwall but if you live in, say, the North of England stop and think before you sign a contract. You will have to stay in Cornwall out of season to avoid the swarms of tourists, the days will be short, the weather uncertain and it may take a very long time to complete your photography. If you are also writing, research will take up an equally lengthy period. If you have an independent income or are being heavily subsidised it could be a delightful assignment, but if not you may well be out of pocket by the time the work is completed.

It sounds unadventurous, but to start with the freelance travel photographer should concentrate if possible on areas he can cover without having to stay away from home, in other words within easy driving or travelling distance since this will cut out the hotel costs which may othewise eat up his profit. Then if successful he may find his publisher is willing to cover the expense of more distant journeys in the future.

Many books, perhaps the majority, are of course illustrated with pictures from many different sources, since the publisher deals with agencies or picture researchers—but this can result in a very uneven result. It is better if the photos represent one person's style, their individual way of looking at a subject, though obtaining a selection from a picture library is probably easier from the publisher's point of view. It is up to you to persuade him that you can do the job more successfully.

Picture Researchers

Many of the major publishers of books, magazines and newspapers employ full-time professional picture researchers whose job it is to find illustrations for books and articles. They have a vast knowledge of sources, are always looking for new ones and once it becomes known that you have an interesting collection of photos of certain subjects you may well be approached.

To work with an experienced researcher is a pleasure. He or she will tell you exactly what subject matter is required, approximately how many pictures are needed, how long they will be kept and give you some idea of the reproduction fee. At the end of the stated period the prints that have not been selected are returned promptly and those that are retained are paid for on publication. Sometimes the cheque is accompanied by a copy of the book or journal. A relationship is built up that can continue for years, with the researcher always asking you first if you can supply the wanted material before other sources are approached.

On the other hand since no qualifications are required anyone can call themselves a picture researcher, a title that sounds interesting and important, and you may encounter inexperienced, unprofessional and occasionally unscrupulous people who will cause much aggravation for little or no return. Often employed on a freelance basis by very small publishing companies, they may be asked for let us say six pictures to illustrate a book on the borders of Kent and Sussex. Not knowing where to find the best sources they write to every landscape photographer whose address they can find asking for all the material he can send on Kent and Sussex, ending up with many hundreds of pictures.

These they keep for a long period, perhaps a year or more, until the book is about to be printed. They then select half a dozen and are faced with returning masses of unused material, and often they don't bother to do this until several angry letters have been received from the photographer. Eventually the people who produced the six pictures used will be sent cheques that hardly cover the cost of production.

It just isn't worth dealing with "researchers" of this type, but it takes experience to detect them. If you send material always accompany it with a letter stating the length of time for which it can be retained, perhaps six weeks, and that after that time you will charge a weekly "holding fee". Talk to as many other photographers as possible to learn which people to deal with and which to avoid—you'll be surprised how many photographers dealing with amateur researchers have lost material forever, the culprit depending on the fact that it isn't worth the time and cost of taking legal action to get it back.

You will inevitably meet with some unfortunate experiences, but once you have found reliable, professional researchers treat them like friends and as you add fresh material to your collection let them know at once so that they can add the knowledge to their records. If you don't possess the pictures they need don't hesitate to suggest other sources if you can—a dog-in-the-manger attitude never pays off.

Calendars, Cards and Posters

You can forget about this section of the market unless you are capable of producing extremely sharp transparencies with good colour saturation, boldly composed and perfectly exposed. The bigger they are the better, only a handful of firms accepting 35mm and some insisting on the 5″ × 4″ format; all the successful photographers in this field are technical experts.

Cards and calendars of outdoor subjects aimed at the mass market should be taken in sunlight with a deep blue sky studded with puffy clouds and with plenty of colourful flowers in the foreground, in other words a town dweller's dream of a country scene. Though very corny, this is what the general public (and therefore the publisher) requires. A few firms aim at people with a more advanced appreciation of pictures but the majority prefer conventional prettiness. A study of the BFP *Market Handbook* will help you to find the best market for your particular type of work.

Posters are another matter, since most of them are aimed at young people and more unconventional and striking subjects are accepted. If you visit a shop selling posters you will get a good idea of what is popular.

All-over sharpness is important, most subjects being taken at a small stop to obtain maximum depth of field, standing the camera on a tripod to avoid even a trace of shake. Some workers use a polarising filter to darken skies still further but most rely on waiting for really good weather; pictures taken on dull or overcast days just don't sell.

Rates vary greatly, some offered by card publishers being far too low. To begin with you may only get a small return from the occasional picture you sell but as you become more aware of the market requirements and build up a useful connection you may start to sell your efforts steadily and may even eventually specialise in this branch.

Copyright

The copyright of a photograph lasts for fifty years and generally speaking the photographer should never part with it unless he is offered a quite exceptional sum—and even then he may live to regret his action. The copyright of written work lasts for fifty years after the death of the author.

The main exception occurs when someone has specially commissioned you to take a certain picture. Someone who has bought a Tudor cottage in a picturesque setting, for instance, may pay you to photograph it and he will then hold the copyright of the result. You must not submit the picture, no matter how saleable, for publication without written permission to do so. On the other hand you will retain the negative and make any further prints required.

Of course, if you are employed by a newspaper, magazine, agency or studio the copyright of any picture taken during the course of your duties belongs to the owner. The same thing usually applies if a freelance is hired for a period to do some work for the firm.

If you deal with card, calender or poster publishers you will probably be asked not to sell your picture for similar use for a period of perhaps five years. This is understandable, but be careful that the agreement you sign does not stop all future publication. Read the small print very carefully before committing yourself to anything and always remember that as Sam Goldwyn so shrewdly remarked, verbal agreements ain't worth the paper they're written on.

Be especially careful if entering a competition run by a commercial firm. A few (luckily the number is in the decline) may state in type so small as to be almost unreadable that if you win a prize you must surrender your negative and the copyright for use by the firm. Since the prize may consist of nothing but a plastic plaque, this is a very cheap way of obtaining pictures for use in advertising and on posters!

You are quite at liberty to include people in pictures intended for publication in books or journals, but you must not use recognisable portraits in advertisements without permission. If, for instance, you had taken a picture of a farmer shearing sheep in which the farmer's face could be clearly seen, it could not be used in an advertisement for sheep-dip unless the farmer agreed, usually in return for a fee. A distant figure in a landscape is another matter and no permission is needed.

Cranbrook Mill, towering above the village in Kent, has probably been photographed since photography was invented. You simply walk along the main street, pause outside a shop, fit a 135 mm lens and include a frame of buildings on either side. However it's easy to get a useless result unless the light and the weather are right. The success of the result will depend on your showing the weather-boarding on the house at the base and making the mill stand out against the sky. On a dull day or with the sun in the wrong position this can't be done, though many amateurs have a go anyway and waste their film.

Legal actions over copyright can drag on and become very complicated, benefiting the lawyers rather than the photographer, so it is always wise if you have any doubts about the position to get a clear, written statement beforehand. Don't assume anything and don't necessarily believe the friendly assurances given over a meal or a drink.

Hobby or Career?

As craftsmanship declines so fewer and fewer people enjoy their work. Bored and frustrated at the office they live only for the weekends when for a short period they can do something that interests them—fishing, pottery, photography, exploring the countryside, sailing, sketching—and then on Monday back to the dreary routine. Why do they do it?

The answer of course is that their work provides them with a regular income with which to pay the mortgage and all the bills with a little left over for a holiday. Many people accept this and are quite content with their lives, which I would look on as so many living deaths. They, on the other hand, might regard the uncertain life of a freelance with horror, asking how he can possibly look after his family and generally pay his way without a steady salary? He must be self-indulgent, self-absorbed, immature, etc, etc.

They may well be right, and I would never encourage anyone to become a full-time freelance photographer of Britain unless they have an independent income or had very good connections in the publishing world, the right temperament—and of course in addition be able to take pictures that interest other people, an item that is often overlooked.

The traditional and safest way of breaking into the game is to have a regular job but to spend your weekends and the summer evenings taking saleable pictures and finding the markets that are available for them. With luck and a lot of very hard work your sales may increase until you reach the point of decision; it looks as though if you worked at photography full time you could earn as much or more as you do at the office. Should you make the break?

A lot of factors must be taken into consideration. Just as an actor may have a successful and well-paid run followed by a long period of unemployment so you may find you sell a lot of pictures during one month and none the next. Your income will fluctuate wildly though your bills remain steady and freelance work calls for a Micawberish optimism.

Secondly, in addition to being fit you have to stay fit since if you can't leave the house you can't take photos and therefore stop earning a living. Carrying a heavy equipment case for long distances over often rough country does call for a certain amount of energy and determination and if you are feeling unwell you can't do it. On the other hand as every office and works manager knows, the more boring the job the greater the incidence of sickness; people do quite genuinely develop coughs, colds and minor ailments if they don't like what they are doing. If you are obsessed with taking pictures of Britain, in other words if you are working at your hobby, you will be surprised how healthy you remain;

colds last half a day, and none of the mysterious aches and pains experienced by bored workers seem to occur.

You have to be blessed with a family that will accept your disappearing at sunrise in summer to return after sunset, muddy and fatigued. They must also be prepared to accept your crazy fluctuations in income; an understanding bank manager who is a keen amateur photographer is a great help.

It is unlikely that you will ever become rich or even well-off simply by photographing Britain but you may well lead a very happy life. A parallel can be drawn with the acting profession in which at any one time 90% of the actors are unemployed, the average yearly income is low and only a handful of people ever become prosperous: common sense tells you to stay out of it and get a regular job instead. In spite of this thousands of young people try to enter the field every year simply because they have a desperate desire to act. Those that succeed often have a hard, impoverished life for many years but they don't mind this because they wouldn't want to do anything else.

If your idea of happiness is to explore the towns, villages and countryside of Britain with a camera and if strangers, not your family and friends, like the pictures you take, then there is a chance that with a great deal of very hard work you could make a career out of your hobby. However, most people would be better advised to stay in the job they already have and add something to their income by freelance work in their spare time. I say this knowing that the really dedicated people, the ones most likely to succeed, will ignore my advice and plunge headfirst into this uncertain and demanding way of earning a living. I wish them a long, happy and lucky life.

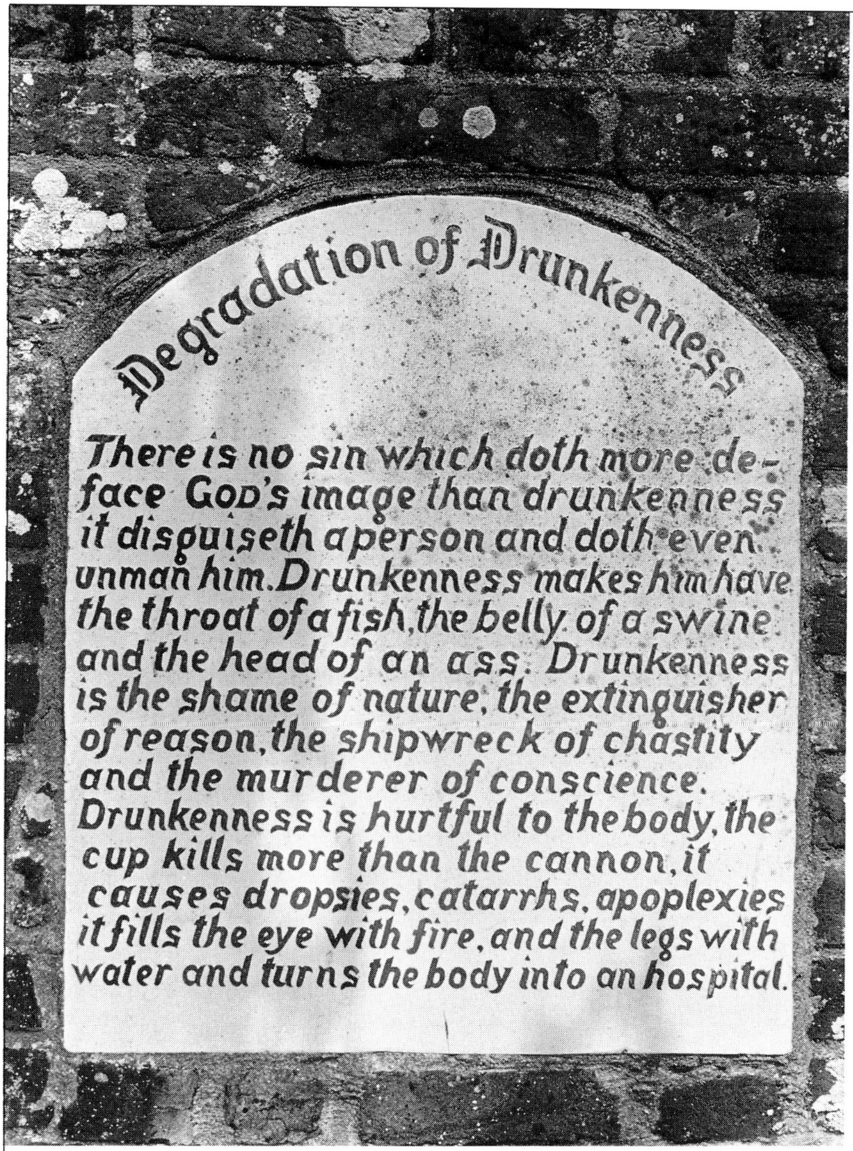

Keep an eye open for odd plaques and notices as you travel around—they sell well. This one, installed by a hard-drinking vicar who presumably was suffering from a hangover, is on a wall at Kirdford in Sussex and is very unevenly lit when the sun shines due to the shadows of tree branches. I had to wait patiently until a cloud made the lighting dull and even before I took the picture. If the subject is static, never take a picture immediately you see it; wait and see if the lighting can be improved.

Useful Addresses

British Association of Picture Libraries & Agencies
13 Woodberry Crescent, London N10 1PJ. Tel: 01-883 2531.

British Ports Association
Commonwealth House, 1–19 New Oxford Street, London WC1A 1DZ. Tel: 01-242 1200.

British Railways Board
P.O.Box 100, Rail House, Euston Square, London NW1 2DZ. Tel: 01-262 3232.

British Tourist Authority/English Tourist Board
Thames Tower, Black's Road, London W6 9EL. Tel: 01-846 9000.

British Waterways Board
Melbury House, Melbury Terrace, London NW1 6JX. Tel: 01-262 6711.

Bureau of Freelance Photographers
Focus House, 497 Green Lanes, London N13 4BP. Tel: 01-882 3315/6.

Central Office of Information
Hercules Road, London SE1 7DU. Tel: 01-928 2345.

Countryside Commission
John Dower House, Cheltenham, Gloucestershire GL50 3RA. Tel: 01-0242 521381.

Countryside Commission for Scotland
Battleby, Redgorton, Perth PH1 3EW. Tel: 0738 27921.

Department of the Environment
2 Marsham Street, London SW1P 3EB. Tel: 01-212 3434.

Forestry Commission
231 Corstophine Road, Edinburgh EH12 7AT. Tel: 031-334 0303.

Historic Buildings & Monuments Commission for England
25 Savile Row, London W1X 2BT. Tel: 01-734 6010.

Historic Buildings & Monuments Directorate
25 Drumsheugh Gardens, Edinburgh EH3 7RN. Tel: 031-226 3611.

Historic Houses Association
10 Charles II Street, London SW1Y 4AA. Tel: 01-839 5345.

Inland Waterways Association
114 Regents Park Road, London NW1 8UQ. Tel: 01-586 2510.

Meteorological Office
London Road, Bracknell, Berkshire RG12 2SZ. Tel: 0344 420242.

National Trust
36 Queen Anne's Gate, London SW1H 9AS. Tel: 01-222 9251.

National Trust for Scotland
5 Charlotte Square, Edinburgh EH2 4DU. Tel: 031-226 5922.

Nature Conservancy Council
19–20 Belgrave Square, London SW1X 8PY. Tel: 01-235 3241.

Northern Ireland Information Service
Stormont Castle, Belfast BT4 3ST. Tel: 0232 63011.

Northern Ireland Tourist Board
River House, 48 High Street, Belfast BT1 2DS. Tel: 0232 231221.

Ordnance Survey
Romsey Road, Maybush, Southampton SO9 4DH. Tel: 0703 775555.

Scottish Information Office
New St Andrews House, Edinburgh EH1 3TD. Tel: 031-556 8400.
Dover House, Whitehall, London SW1A. Tel: 01-233 3000.

Scottish Tourist Board
23 Ravelston Terrace, Edinburgh EH4 3EU. Tel: 031-332 2433.

Wales Tourist Board
Brunel House, 2 Fitzalan Road, Cardiff CF2 1UY. Tel: 0222 499909.

Welsh Office
Information Division, Cathays Park, Cardiff CF1 3NQ. Tel: 0222 825111.

About the BFP

Founded in 1965, the Bureau of Freelance Photographers is today the major body for the freelance photographer. It has a worldwide membership of some 10,000, comprising not only full-time freelances, but also amateur and semi-professional photographers. Being primarily a service organisation, membership of the Bureau is open to anyone with an interest in freelance photography.

The major service offered to members is the *Market Newsletter*, a confidential monthly report on the state of the freelance market. A well-researched and highly authoritative publication, the *Newsletter* keeps freelances in touch with the market for freelance pictures. It gives full information on the type of pictures currently being sought by a wide range of publications and other outlets. It gives details of new magazines and their editorial requirements, and generally reports on what is happening in the publishing world and how this is likely to affect the freelance photographer. The *Newsletter* is considered essential reading for the freelance and aspiring freelance photographer, and because it pinpoints changes in the marketplace as they occur, it also acts as a useful supplement to the *Handbook*. The *Handbook* itself is now an integral part of BFP membership services; members paying the full annual fee automatically receive a copy every year as it is published.

Other services provided to members for the modest annual subscription include:

● Advisory service. Individual advice on all aspects of freelancing is available to members.

● Fee Recovery Service. The Bureau tries to protect its members' interests in every way it can. In particular, it has been able to assist individual members in recovering unpaid reproduction fees.

● Exclusive Items and Special Offers. The Bureau regularly offers books and other items, usually at discount prices. It originated Contributor's Submission Forms for use by members, and is also able to supply Model Release Forms. In addition, under the Photographic Services & Supplies section of the *Handbook* can be found a number of companies providing special discounts to BFP members on production of a current membership card.

Further Reading

The Business of Freelancing
by Graham Jones
Published by BFP Books, Focus House, 497 Green Lanes, London N13 4BP.
A comprehensive guide to the business side of freelance writing and photography. Contains detailed advice on business organisation, research, finance, and legal matters, plus plenty of ideas for business expansion and maximising profits.

Freelance Photographer's Market Handbook
Published by the Bureau of Freelance Photographers, Focus House, 497 Green Lanes, London N13 4BP.
An annual publication containing detailed listings of markets for photographs and illustrated articles. Market areas covered in depth include consumer magazines, trade magazines, picture agencies and libraries, and greetings card and calendar publishers. Also includes useful articles on approaching the market, and a directory of companies offering photographic services and supplies. The Handbook is included within membership of the Bureau of Freelance Photographers, or can be purchased separately.

The Photographer & the Law
by Don Cassell
Published by BFP Books, Focus House, 497 Green Lanes, London N13 4BP.
A complete guide to the legal aspects of photography. Of most interest to the photographer who is out and about in Britain, there is full information on the law relating to trespass, privacy, and other aspects of the rights and obligations of the photographer in public places. Also contains detailed information on copyright, libel, wildlife photography, insurance, and the rights of the photographer as consumer. Written in clear language easily understandable by the layman.

Photographer's Guides to London, Kent and Sussex
by Kevin MacDonnell Published by Wildwood House, Gower House, Croft Road, Aldershot, Hants GU11 3HR.
Written by the author of 'Freelance Photographers' Britain', these guides to specific parts

of the country point out the many places of photographic interest in those parts of the country, as well as supplying plenty of information about more off-beat subjects that might otherwise be overlooked.

Writing for Profit
by John Wade
Published by BFP Books, Focus House, 497 Green Lanes, London N13 4BP.
Shows how to add words to your pictures to improve their saleability, from simple caption writing to writing and producing your own book. It shows how to find ideas for articles, how to research them, and how to write the final piece. It also discusses the 'tools of the trade', how to analyse markets and how to conduct interviews.

Writers' & Artists' Yearbook
Published by A & C Black, 35 Bedford Row, London WC1R 4JH.
Annual publication containing a detailed listing of leading book publishers and the subjects they cover. Also contains useful information on literary agents, editorial services, copyright, picture agencies and other useful addresses, but with the writer rather than the photographer in mind.

Index